THE OUTSIDERS

S. E. Hinton

AUTHORED by Meghan Joyce
UPDATED AND REVISED by Damien Chazelle

COVER DESIGN by Table XI Partners LLC
COVER PHOTO by Olivia Verma and © 2005 GradeSaver, LLC

BOOK DESIGN by Table XI Partners LLC

Published by GradeSaver LLC, www.gradesaver.com

First published in the United States of America by GradeSaver LLC. 2009

GRADESAVER, the GradeSaver logo and the phrase "Getting you the grade
since 1999" are registered trademarks of GradeSaver, LLC

ISBN 978-1-60259-178-3

Printed in the United States of America

For other products and additional information please visit
http://www.gradesaver.com

Table of Contents

Table of Contents

Biography of Hinton, S. E. (1950-)

Susan Eloise Hinton was born in Tulsa, Oklahoma on July 22, 1950. She earned her B.S. degree from the University of Tulsa in 1970. *The Outsiders*, her first novel, was published by Viking in 1967 when Hinton was just seventeen years old.

After three years of writer's block, she published *That Was Then, This Is Now* in 1971 by writing two pages every day. The summer before, she had married David Inhofe. Hinton's shortest novel, *Rumble Fish*, was published in 1975. It had previously been published as a short story in a 1968 edition of *Nimrod*, the literary supplement for the *University of Tulsa Alumni Magazine*. *Tex* was published in 1979. Hinton didn't publish another book until *Taming the Star Runner* in 1988.

In August of 1983, Hinton's son, Nick, was born. In 1988, Hinton became the first recipient of the Young Adult Services Division of the American Library Association and School Library Journal Author Achievement Award. Other awards include the Margaret A. Edwards Award in 1989, also from the Young Adult Library Services Association, and the Arrell Gibson Lifetime Achievement Award from the Oklahoma Center for the Book in 1997.

Hinton has written two children's books: *Big David, Little David*, published in 1995, and her most recent book, *The Puppy Sister*.

About The Outsiders

Published in 1967 by Viking Press, *The Outsiders* was S.E. Hinton's first novel. The rivalry between the "greasers" and the "socs" was based on events in her own high school, the Will Rogers High School in Tulsa, Oklahoma. Hinton began writing the novel during her sophomore year, and it was published when she was just seventeen years old. Hinton says of the inspiration behind the story:

> "One day, a friend of mine was walking home from school and these "nice" kids jumped out of a car and beat him up because they didn't like him being a greaser. This made me mad and I just went home and started pounding out a story about this boy who was beaten up while he was walking home from the movies - the beginning of *The Outsiders.*"

When it was released, *The Outsiders'* portrayal of juvenile delinquents caused controversy. However, it was wildly popular among young adults, selling over four million copies in the United States. *The Outsiders* earned such publicity that the pressure caused Hinton to suffer from three years of writer's block.

Over the years, *The Outsiders* has won various awards, including making the New York Herald Tribune Best Teenage Books List and the Chicago Tribune Book World Spring Book Festival Honor Book, both in 1967. It also won the Media and Methods Maxi Award and was named one of the ALA Best Young Adult Books, both in 1975. In 1979, it won the Massachusetts Children's Book Award.

A film version was produced in 1983, directed by Francis Ford Coppola. It featured C. Thomas Howell as Ponyboy, Rob Lowe as Soda, Emilo Estevez as Two-Bit Mathews, Matt Dillon as Dally Winston, Tom Cruise as Steve Randle, Patrick Swayze as Darry, Ralph Macchio as Johnny Cade, and Diane Lane as Cherry Valance.

Character List

Ponyboy

The narrator of [I]The Outsiders, Ponyboy is fourteen years old and a greaser. He has "light-brown, almost-red hair and greenish-gray eyes," and wears his hair "longer than a lot of boys wear theirs, squared off in the back and long at the front and sides."

Soda

Ponyboy's second-oldest brother, who is sixteen. Ponyboy describes him as "always happy-go-lucky and grinning." He is extraordinarily handsome with a "finely drawn, sensitive face that somehow manages to be reckless and thoughtful at the same time."

Darry

Ponyboy's oldest brother, who is twenty. He works as a roofer. Ponyboy describes him as someone who is "hard and firm and rarely grins at all," in contrast to Soda. He has "grown up too fast." He was the captain of the football team in high school and won a college scholarship, but had to work to take care of the family.

Two-Bit Mathews

Two-Bit, whose real name is Keith, earned his nickname because "you couldn't shut that guy up; he always had to get hsi two-bits worth in." He is the oldest member of the the greaser gang, and "the wisecracker of the bunch." He is famous for shop-lifting everything he can, including his black-handled switchblade, which he is also known for. As Ponyboy describes him, "He was about six feet tall, stocky in build, and very proud of his long rusty-colored sideburns. He had gray eyes and a wide grin, and he couldn't stop making funny remarks to save his life... He liked fights, blondes, and for some unfathomable reason, school."

Dally

Dally's real name is Dallas Winston, and he is the toughest member of the greaser gang. Ponyboy describes him as having "an elfish face, with high cheekbones and a pointed chin, small, sharp animal teeth, and ears like a lynx. His hair was almost white it was so blond, and he didn't like haircuts, or hair oil either, so it fell over his forehead in wisps and kicked out in the back in tufts and curled behind his ears and along the nape of his neck. His eyes were blue, blazing ice, cold with a hatred of the whole world."

He is a jockey, and surprisingly doesn't fix races; it's "the only thing Dally did honestly." Although he is only seventeen years old, "the fight for self-preservation had hardened him beyond caring."

Johnny

Johnny Cade is the second-youngest in the greaser gang, besides Ponyboy. He is "smaller than the rest, with a slight build. He had big black eyes in a dark tanned face; his hair was jet-black and heavily greased and combed to the side, but it was so long that it fell in shaggy bangs across his forehead. He had a nervous, suspicious look in his eyes... He was the gang's pet, everyone's kid brother."

But after being beaten badly by the Socs four months before the action of the story commences, he is "jumpier than ever." He was always "high-strung," living in a household where his parents beat him all the time. When the Socs attack him and Ponyboy, he kills Bob to stop them from drowning Ponyboy.

Sandy

Soda's girlfriend. "Her hair was natural blond and her laugh was soft, like her china-blue eyes. She didn't have a real good home or anything and was our kind-greaser-but she was a real nice girl."

Steve Randle

Soda's best friend, but Ponyboy doesn't like him much. He is "seventeen, tall and lean," cocky, and smart.

Father

Ponyboy's father died in a car accident eight months ago. He remembers his father as looking just like Darry, with "dark-brown hair that kicks out in front and a slight cowlick in the back."

Evie

Steve Randle's girlfriend. She cried when Steve went to jail, before the story starts.

Cherry Valance

Cherry is a redhead Soc girl, Bob's girlfriend, whom Ponyboy meets at the drive-in when Dally is bothering her and Marcia. In their first one-on-one interaction, Ponyboy realizes how much principle means to Cherry: "Cherry had said she wouldn't drink Dally's Coke if she was starving, and she meant it. It was the principle of the thing. But Marcia saw no reason to throw away a perfectly good, free Coke."

Marcia

Cherry Valance's friend, whom Ponyboy and Johnny meet at the drive-in theater. She is "a little smaller than Cherry" and "cute," with "short dark hair."

Sylvia

Dally's sometime girlfriend. When he was in reform school, she had "started hanging onto Johnny and sweet-talking him," but Steve told her to stay away from Johnny for Johnny's sake. In Chapter 1, we find out that Dally has broken up with her for cheating on him while he was in jail.

Bob Sheldon

Cherry Valance's Soc boyfriend, whom Johnny Cade kills to defend Ponyboy. He is handsome, with black hair, and wears three heavy rings; he used them before the story started to cut up Johnny's face.

Randy Adderson

Marcia's Soc boyfriend, and Bob's best friend. He is "a tall guy with a semi-Beatle haircut."

Mom

Ponyboy's Mom was killed in a car accident eight months ago, with his Father. She had the ability to make people smile no matter what. She used to be able to talk to Dally Winston and keep him out of trouble. Ponyboy describes her as "golden and beautiful..."

David

One of Bob and Randy's friends, he is the Soc who tries to drown Ponyboy in the fountain in Chapter 4.

Buck Merril

Dally's rodeo partner, in his mid-twenties, a "tall lanky cowboy with blond hair," who used to have buckteeth before they were knocked out in a fight. Ponyboy and Johnny find Dally at Buck's house the night Johnny kills Bob. He loves Hank Williams.

Jerry Wood

One of the schoolteachers who was picnicking with children when the church caught on fire. He stays with Ponyboy in the hospital, and doesn't "seem to mind our being hoods."

Mrs. O'Brient

One of the schoolteachers who was picnicking with the children when the church caught on fire.

Curly Shepard

Tim Shepard's little brother, "a tough, cool, hard-as-nails Tim in miniature... an average downtown hood, tough and not real bright." At the time of the rumble, he is in the reformatory.

Tim Shepard

The leader of the other main Greaser gang. He is a "lean, catlike eighteen-year-old who looked like the model JD you see in movies and magazines. He had the right curly black hair, smoldering dark eyes, and a long scar from temple to chin where a tramp had belted him with a broken pop bottle. He had a tough, hard look to him and his nose had been broken twice." Ponyboy compares him to Dally because they both like being hoods, and because they have the same "grim and bitter" smile.

Mr. Syme

Ponyboy's English teacher, who assigns the semester theme that becomes *The Outsiders*.

Major Themes

The Socs vs. Greasers

The conflict between Socs and Greasers is introduced in Chapter 1, and escalates throughout the book. The Greasers are "poorer than the Socs and the middle class... almost like hoods; we steal things and rive old souped-up cars and hold up gas stations and have a gang fight once in a while." In contrast, the Socs are "the jet set, the West-side rich kids," who "jump greasers and wreck houses and throw beer blasts for kicks, and get editorials in the paper for being a public disgrace one day and an asset to society the next."

In Chapter 3, a conversation between Ponyboy and Cherry defines a distinction between the two groups that goes beyond money. Cherry says, "You greasers have a different set of values. You're more emotional. We're sophisticated - cool to the point of not feeling anything. Nothing is real with us." And Ponyboy agrees that "It's not money, it's feeling - you don't feel anything and we feel too violently."

In Chapter 7, as he explains why he is leaving town instead of attending the rumble, Randy explains the lose-lose situation to Ponyboy:

> "You can't win, even if you whip us. You'll still be where you were before - at the bottom. And we'll still be the lucky ones with all the breaks. So it doesn't do any good, the fighting and the killing. It doesn't prove a thing. We'll forget it if you win, or if you don't. Greasers will still be greasers and Socs will still be Socs."

The theme of appearances is linked to the conflict between the Socs and the Greasers, and its importance is underlined when the Socs arrive at the rumble in Chapter 9. Ponyboy realizes that the reason the Socs never get blamed for causing trouble is because "We look hoody and they look decent." Although most of the Greasers are "pretty decent guys underneath all that grease," and the Socs are "just cold-blooded mean," it doesn't matter because "people usually go by looks."

Hair

The Greasers' hairstyle is what distinguishes them as hoods, and part of the appearance that keeps them relegated to the margins of society. Ponyboy demonstrates his belief in hair's importance by including it in his character descriptions. In the first paragraph of Chapter 1, he says, "I have light-brown, almost-red hair... longer than a lot of boys wear theirs, squared off in back and long at the front and sides, but I am a greaser and most of my neighborhood rarely bothers to get a haircut."

His hair is his pride and joy, and it is a painful identity change for him to cut it off when he and Johnny try to disguise themselves. When Johnny reveals his plan to cut it, Ponyboy narrates, "It was my pride. It was long and silky, just like Soda's only a little redder. Our hair was tuff - we didn't have to use much grease on it. Our hair labeled us greasers, too - it was our trademark. The one thing we were proud of. Maybe we couldn't have Corvairs or madras shirts, but we could have hair."

In contrast to Ponyboy and Soda, Darry keeps his hair short. It is a demonstration of his resentment of his role as a Greaser -- as if he doesn't belong in that place in society.

Eyes

Characters' eyes are used to demonstrate their emotions, and Ponyboy frequently draws attention to them. He himself has "greenish-gray eyes."

Ponyboy's view of other characters is often tied to his interpretation of their eyes; for example, he says that "Darry's eyes are his own. He's got eyes that are like two pieces of pale blue-green ice. They've got a determined set to them, like the rest of him... he would be real handsome if his eyes weren't so cold." Darry's eyes reflect Ponyboy's view of his oldest brother as "hardly human." In contrast, Sodapop's eyes are "dark brown - lively, dancing, recklessly laughing eyes that can be gentle and sympathetic one moment and blazing with anger the next."

Johnny's eyes in particular are used to reflect his emotions; for instance, when the Socs approach, his terror is always apparent in his eyes. The difference between his mother and him is clear to Ponyboy because of their eyes: "Johnnycake's eyes were fearful and sensitive; hers were cheap and hard."

Appearances

Ponyboy is very conscious of the way he and others look. It is clear in his descriptions of people as a narrator, but also in his interactions with the world. For example, in Chapter 1, when the Socs start to surround him, he "automatically hitched my thumbs in my jeans and slouched" to appear tougher. In Chapter 3, when the Socs stop the boys with Cherry and Marcia, "Two-bit took a long drag on his cigarette, Johnny slouched and hooked his thumbs in his pockets, and I stiffened." Ponyboy notes that, "We can look meaner than anything when we want to - looking tough comes in handy."

In Chapter 4, when the boys are going to ask for directions to Jay Mountain, Ponyboy sees Johnny "as a stranger might see him," and realizes that they will never pass for farm boys. He thinks, "They'll know we're hoods the minute they see us." Even though he knows Johnny is kind and gentle, "he looked hard and tough, because of his black T-shirt and his blue jeans and jacket, and because his hair was heavily greased and so long." Johnny notices the same thing about Ponyboy and tells him to "quit slouching down like a thug."

This theme is closely tied to the theme of hair as a defining characteristic for the Greasers. In Chapter 7, Ponyboy confesses, "I'd die if I got my picture in the paper with my hair looking so lousy."

As the gang leaves the house to go to the rumble in Chapter 9, Soda begins the role playing game by shouting: "I am a greaser. I am a JD and a hood. I blacken the name of our fair city. I beat up people. I rob gas stations. I am a menace to society. Man, do I have fun!" The game allows the gang mebers to get excited about their rumble, but at the same time reveals how conscious they are of their appearance to the rest of society. Appearance is what defines them and what sets them apart; it is both boon and stumbling block.

Sunsets

Ponyboy and Cherry like to watch sunsets, and they discover they have this in common in their conversation in Chapter 3. Ponyboy thinks, "It seemed funny to me that the sunset she saw from her patio and the one I saw from the back steps was the same one. Maybe the two different worlds we lived in weren't so different. We saw the same sunset." In Chapter 8, after Cherry says she cannot go visit Johnny in the hospital because he is the one who killed her boyfriend, Bob, Ponyboy yells at her and tells her he doesn't want her charity. After she apologizes, he lets her know he still feels a connection to her that bridges their social statuses by asking, "can you see the sunset real good from the West Side?" She is surprised, but answers yes. He says, "You can see it good from the East Side, too."

Watching the sunset becomes a link between the world of the Greasers and that of the Socs, and also hints at the kind of personality that questions things, that is always searching, that is in a way poetic.

In Chapter 7, Randy joins the ranks of those who appreciate sunsets. Ponyboy realizes, "Cherry had said her friends were too cool to feel anything, and yet she could remember watching sunsets. Randy was supposed to be too cool to feel anything, and yet there was pain in his eyes."

The Country

In Chapter 3, while Ponyboy and Johnny lie in the vacant lot watching the stars, Ponyboy dreams of the country as a place where everything is right in the world. In his fantasy, his parents are alive again, and Darry no longer has that "cold, hard look;" he is "like he used to be, eight months ago, before Mom and Dad were killed." Johnny comes to live with Ponyboy's family in the county, and Ponyboy's mother even convinces Dally Winston that "there was some good in the world after all."

The reason the country appeals to Ponyboy so much is because, "I only wanted to lie on my back under a tree and read a book or draw a picture, and not worry about being jumped or carrying a blade or ending up married to some scatterbrained broad with no sense."

In Chapter 4, when the boys jump off the train in Windrixville, Ponyboy notices that "the clouds were pink and meadow larks were singing." He thinks to himself, "This is the country... My dream's come true and I'm in the country." But later, as he looks for someone to ask directions from, he thinks to himself, "I was in the country, but I knew I wasn't going to like it as much as I'd thought I would."

Pretending

Ponyboy often creates alternate realities for himself to cope with situations that he feels are unbearable. For instance, while he and Johnny watch the starts in the vacant lot in Chapter 3, he thinks, "I felt the tension growing inside of me and I knew something had to happen or I would explode." In response, he dreams about a life in the country where his parents are still alive and Darry is kind again.

He is also good at pretending when it comes to lying, and lies easily to the farmer when he asks how to get to Jay Mountain. He thinks, "I can lie so easily that it spooks me sometimes." In this case, he is creating an alternate reality to cover the fact that he and Johnny are hiding away after having committed murder.

Ponyboy is conscious of his tendency to pretend, and even his preference for his dreams over reality. In Chapter 5, he admits, "I liked my books and clouds and sunsets. Dally was so real he scared me."

Chapter 10 begins with the most obvious case yet of pretending: Ponyboy cannot grasp that Johnny has died, so he tells himself, "That still body back in the hospital wasn't Johnny." He pretends that he'll find Johnny at the house, or in the lot. This case of denial has been foreshadowed by Ponyboy's tendency to create alternate realities for himself throughout the story, but the difference is that "this time my dreaming worked. I convinced myself that he wasn't dead."

Gone with the Wind

Johnny buys this book for Ponyboy when they are staying in the abandoned church, and they kill time by reading it. Johnny doesn't understand a lot about the Civil War, but he is obsessed with the idea of southern gentlemen, "impressed with their manners and charm." He compares them to Dally, showing how he idolizes Dally even though Ponyboy doesn't see much to respect in him at the time.

When Ponyboy and Two-Bit go to visit Johnny in the hospital, he asks them to buy him a new copy of *Gone with the Wind,* since the old one burned in the church. When Johnny dies, he leaves his copy of the book to Ponyboy. Ponyboy links Johnny and Dally's deaths to *Gone with the Wind,* as he considers how they "died gallant." He can only think of "Southern gentlemen with big black eyes in blue jeans and T-shirts, Southern gentlemen crumpling under street lights."

Glossary of Terms

A'woofin'
Kidding or teasing

Bopper
Rumbler, or fighter, to the Brumly gang

Bum
Used as an adjective to mean wretched, worthless

Corn-poney
Unsophisticated, corny

Crocked
Drunk

Dig
Understand, appreciate

Heater
Gun

Holler uncle
Give up

Madras
A light, cotton fabric of various weaves, used for shirts.

One-horse
Small and insignificant

Pickled
Drunk

Rank
Used as an adjective to mean inferior

Reformatory
A correctional institution for minors

Savvy?

"Understand?"

Snooker

A game that is a variant of pool, played with 15 red balls (with a point value of 1) and 6 balls of other colors (with point values from 2 to 7).

Soft

Delicate, not a good fighter

Switch

Short for switchblade, a type of pocketknife.

Tagalong

A person who follows another's lead.

Tuff

Different from "tough," which means rough; "tuff" means "cool, sharp."

Weed

Cigarette

Short Summary

Ponyboy Curtis, the fourteen-year-old narrator, lives with his older brothers Sodapop and Darry, since their parents passed away in a car accident. They are all members of a Greaser gang, meaning they are considered hoods or juvenile delinquents by society. Other than being financially and socially disadvantaged, the Greasers' main problem is getting jumped by the Socs, the rich kids from the West Side. The other members of the Greaser gang are Johnny Cade, Dally Winston, Two-Bit Mathews, and Steve Randle.

One night at the drive-in theater, Ponyboy, Johnny, Two-Bit, and Dally meet Cherry Valance and Marcia, two Soc girls whose boyfriends have left them there. Ponyboy makes a connection with Cherry because they can both appreciate sunsets; it is a bond that crosses their social boundaries and links their worlds. On the walk home, Bob Sheldon and Randy Adderson, the girls' boyfriends, accost the group and take the girls home.

Later that night, Ponyboy and Johnny accidentally fall asleep in their favorite vacant lot. Ponyboy runs home, but when Darry scolds him and hits him for the first time, he goes back to find Johnny. They are jumped by Bob, Randy, and other Socs, and during the fight Johnny stabs and kills Bob to stop him from drowning Ponyboy in a fountain. Panicked, Ponyboy and Johnny find Dally, who they know will help them. He gives them some money and a gun and tells them to get on a train to Windrixville and hide out in a deserted church.

Ponyboy and Johnny stay at the church for about a week, during which time they cut off their long Greaser hair as a disguise and subsist mainly on baloney. Dally comes to meet them eventually, and takes them out to get burgers. While they are out, Johnny decides to turn himself in. But when the characters get back to the church, they find it's on fire. A school group had been having a picnic there, and some children are trapped inside. Ponyboy and Johnny run in and save the children, but Johnny is caught across the back by a burning piece of timber.

Soda and Darry come to the hospital to pick up Ponyboy, and they learn that Dally's arm is burned and Johnny is in critical condition. The boys go home because there is a rumble against the Socs that they need to attend. Ponyboy feels sick, but decides to go to the rumble anyway. Dally escapes from the hospital to fight in the rumble, and the Greasers win.

Dally takes Ponyboy back to the hospital to visit Johnny, who is dying. Before he dies, Johnny tells Ponyboy, "Stay gold," meaning he shouldn't lose the innocence of childhood, and should avoid becoming hardened like Dally. Dally is extremely emotional after Johnny's death, since he loved Johnny, and runs off. Ponyboy is feeling even sicker, but has to go home and tell the rest of the gang that Johnny is dead.

Dally calls the Curtis house from a payphone to say that he's robbed a grocery store and the cops are chasing him. The whole gang runs to the vacant lot, and sees Dally approaching from the other side, followed by cop cars. Dally pulls out his gun on the cops, and they shoot him, killing him. Ponyboy passes out and is delirious and sick for the rest of the weekend.

He wakes up in bed, and is in denial over Johnny's death. He has to go to court to testify about the events surrounding it, and is acquitted and allowed to continue living with Darry and Soda, rather than being sent to a boys' home. But things are not the same for him; his world is upside-down, and his grades start to slip. Darry confronts Ponyboy and brings up his failing grades, and a huge fight commences between them. Soda is upset by all the fighting, and runs out of the house.

Darry and Ponyboy find Soda in the vacant lot, and he tells them he can't stand how they fight all the time, since they'll only survive if they stick together. All they have is each other. Darry and Ponyboy hadn't realized their fighting upset Soda so much, and they vow to get along and take care of each other. Ponyboy has to decide what to write about for his semester theme in English class, and he decides to write *The Outsiders* as a warning to other boys at risk to turn their lives around before it's too late.

Quotes and Analysis

"How'd you like that haircut to begin just below the chin?"

An anonymous Soc says this to Ponyboy in Chapter 1

The Socs have jumped Ponyboy, and are taunting him about his hair. At this point, they are holding him down with a knife at his throat. The phrase is not just a threat of violence (it implies the Soc is about to slit Ponyboy's throat), but a reference to the distinguishing quality that makes Ponyboy stand out as a Greaser: his hair.

"Things are rough all over."

Cherry Valance says this to Ponyboy in Chapter 2

Ponyboy has just finished relating the story of Johnny's attack to Cherry, and to the reader for the first time. Cherry is shocked, but points out to him that not all Socs act that way, just like not all Greasers act like Dally. She insists that "We have troubles you've never even heard of."

In Chapter 7, as Randy tells Ponyboy that he is tired of fighting and is going to leave town instead of going to the rumble, Ponyboy remembers Cherry saying "Things are rough all over," and understands what she meant. By the end of the chapter, Ponyboy has decided that, "Things were rough all over, but it was better that way. That way you could tell the other guy was human too."

"Maybe the two different worlds we lived in weren't so different. We saw the same sunset."

Ponyboy as narrator in Chapter 3

After talking to Cherry and realizing he can really connect with her, Ponyboy uses the sunset as a bridge between the world of the Greasers and that of the Socs. Throughout the story, he notices the sunset and thinks of Cherry, and notes that she is seeing the same sunset. This daily natural occurrence links two disparate worlds -- and the implication is that it links far more as well.

"Next time you want a broad, pick up your own kind."

Bob says this to Johnny and Ponyboy in Chapter 3

Right before the Socs attack Ponyboy and Johnny, in the fight that results in Johnny killing Bob, Bob describes the reasoning for the attack. He wants the Greasers to know their place in society, and to stay away from Soc girls. Later, in Chapter 6, Dallas Winston echos Bob's words when he explains how Cherry is acting as a spy for the Greasers, saying, "Man, next time I want a broad I'll pick up my own kind." Ponyboy remembers Bob saying this, and a link is created between Bob and Dally, both of whom die young before the story ends.

"You can't win, even if you whip us. You'll still be where you were before - at the bottom. And we'll still be the lucky ones with all the breaks. So it doesn't do any good, the fighting and the killing. It doesn't prove a thing. We'll forget it if you win, or if you don't. Greasers will still be greasers and Socs will still be Socs."

Randy says this to Ponyboy in Chapter 7

This speech describes the plight of the Greasers, and the futility of fighting. Randy has decided to leave town instead of attending the rumble that night, and here he explains to Ponyboy why. Fighting and killing don't solve anything; the gap between social classes remains, and continues to define the Greasers and the Socs.

"I am a greaser. I am a JD and a hood. I blacken the name of our fair city. I beat up people. I rob gas stations. I am a menace to society. Man, do I have fun!"

Soda chants this as they leave the house for the rumble in Chapter 9

This chant begins the role-playing game, in which Two-Bit and Darry pretend to be Socs. The game allows them to get excited about their rumble, but at the same time reveals how conscious they are of their appearance to the rest of society. Though not all of the stereotypes are true of all Greasers, they embrace their appearance, refracting to a degree what they feel society thinks of them.

"Stay gold, Ponyboy. Stay gold..."

Johnny whispers this to Ponyboy before he dies in Chapter 9

In his last words, Johnny references the same Robert Frost poem that Ponyboy recited aloud when they were sitting on the back porch of the church, watching the sunrise. By dying, Johnny fulfills the prophecy of the poem that "Nothing gold can stay." But he wishes that Ponyboy would fulfill his own potential by not becoming a convict and using his intelligence to get out of the hood.

"We're all we've got left. We ought to be able to stick together against everything. If we don't have each other, we don't have anything."

Ponyboy and Darry's relationship has been strained since their parents died and Darry became responsible for his little brothers. They fight all the time, and throughout the story try to reconcile and come to an understanding. But they never think of how their fighting affects Soda until Chapter 12, when he runs out of the house. When they catch him in the park, he tells them the above quote, pointing out the unity that defines their family now.

"I've been thinking about it, and that poem, that guy that wrote it, he meant you're gold when you're a kid, like green. When you're a kid everything's new, dawn. It's just when you get used to everything that it's day. Like the way you dig sunsets, Pony. That's gold. Keep that way, it's a good way to be."

This is an excerpt from the note Johnny writes Ponyboy, which Ponyboy reads in Chapter 12

This quotation is Johnny's explanation of his own last words, "Stay gold." Reading this note inspires Ponyboy to write *The Outsiders* as his semester theme for English class. In the note, Johnny says to "tell Dally" about staying gold, but Ponyboy knows it is too late, since Dally is already dead by the time he reads it. So Ponyboy feels compelled to share what he has learned from his own experience as a Greaser with others, so that the fighting might stop and lives might be saved.

Summary and Analysis of Chapters 1 and 2

Summary

The novel begins with Ponyboy, the narrator, leaving the "darkness of the movie house." He has just seen a Paul Newman film. He describes himself for the reader, physically, and notes his household situation: he lives with his older brothers, Darry and Soda. Their parents were killed in a car accident, and the boys can "stay together only as long as we behave." He also describes his social status, which is that of a "Greaser".

Ponyboy grows nervous that he's walking alone, since Greasers often get jumped by Socs, "the jet set, the West-side rich kids." As soon as he has this thought, a red Corvair starts following him, and he starts sweating and getting scared. Soon he is surrounded by Socs. One of them flips out a knife and asks if Ponyboy needs a haircut; he is overpowered by them, with the knife to his throat, and starts screaming.

A scuffle ensues, and Ponyboy is helped to his feet by Darry, his oldest brother. The Greaser gang has chased away the Socs. Sodapop, Ponyboy's other older brother, comforts him as he cries, and soon the whole gang comes back. They've chased the Socs away with rocks. Ponyboy describes Steve Randle, Two-bit Mathews, Dallas Winston, and Johnny Cade to the reader; they compose the Greaser gang.

Ponyboy is bleeding where the Soc cut his face. Soon Darry starts scolding Ponyboy for walking home from the movies by himself, and Ponyboy explains to the reader that "Me and Darry just didn't dig each other. I never could please him." Soda sticks up for Ponyboy, as he usually does. Dally suggests going to the movies the next night, but Steve and Soda have plans with their girlfriends, Evie and Sandy. Ponyboy says he and Johnny will go to the movies, then starts to ponder the type of girls the Greasers end up with. He wonders if other girls act the same.

Later that night, Ponyboy is reading *Great Expectations* for school, and relates to Pip, the main character. He remembers a time in biology when a cute girl was startled when he flipped out his knife to dissect a worm. Meanwhile, Soda is giving Darry a back massage for a pulled muscle from his job roofing. Ponyboy bemons how Darry has to "work like an old man when he was twenty," just to take care of his brothers.

Sodapop comes to bed, and explains to Ponyboy that Darry "don't mean nothin'. He's just got more worries than somebody his age ought to." Ponyboy doesn't really understand, though. They talk about why Soda dropped out of school: "'Cause I'm dumb." Soda says he's going to marry Sandy, his girlfriend, in the near future when she finishes school. He tells Ponyboy he's in love with her, and then falls asleep. The chapter ends with Ponyboy wondering what Soda meant about Darry. He finds it hard to believe that his oldest brother loves him, when he's always scolding him. He tells himself he doesn't care about his relationship with Darry, but admits that, "I lie to myself all the time. But I never believe me."

Chapter 2 begins the next night, when Johnny and Ponyboy meet up with Dally to go to a movie. They get there early, and have time to shoplift cigarettes from the drugstore. They arrive at The Dingo, "a pretty rough hangout," and catch up on "who was running away, and who was in jail, and who was going with who, and who could whip who, and who stole what and when and why." On the way to the drive-in theater, they cause trouble chasing around junior high kids. Then they sneak in over the back fence of the Nightly Double drive-in movie, even though they have enough money to get in.

Dally walks down the aisle and sits right behind the only two other people there: two Soc girls, "dressed sharp and real good-looking." Dally taunts them even though they ask him to leave them alone, and the redhead, whose name is Cherry Valance, threatens to call the cops. Dally goes off to buy Cokes, and the girls see Ponyboy and Johnny. Their demeanor immediately changes, and they are friendly to the two younger, less-threatening boys. Ponyboy remembers that Cherry is a cheerleader at his school.

Cherry, her friend, Marcia, and Ponyboy strike up a conversation, and Cherry asks about Soda, because she knows he works at the gas station. Ponyboy admits that Soda dropped out of school, a fact that embarrasses him for his brother. Johnny returns, and is clearly nervous around the girls. Soon Dally comes back with Cokes, but Cherry throws hers in his face. Dally "smiled dangerously," and gears up to harass her some more, but Johnny reaches out and stops him. Ponyboy notes that Johnny is the only one of the gang who could stand up to Dally without getting punched, since "he was the gang's pet." Instead, Dally storms away and doesn't return.

The girls invite Ponyboy and Johnny to stay with them, to protect them. Cherry points out that she notices a huge difference between them and Dally; they're not "dirty." But she does say that she admires Dally. Ponyboy soon learns that the girls had come with their boyfriends, but had left them when they realized the boys were getting drunk.

Two-bit sneaks up on the characters, pretending to be a Soc, and really scares Johnny, whose "eyes were shut and [who] was white as a ghost." (Johnny has recently been jumped by Socs and hurt extremely badly, but Two-bit forgot.) Two-bit starts to flirt with Marcia, and updates them on Dally's whereabouts: Timothy Shepard, the leader of the other major Greaser gang, is looking for Dally because Dally slashed his car's tires. They talk about the impending fight, and Cherry is taken aback at their nonchalant approach to violence. Two-bit explains that that's what happens when you get caught: "Our one rule, besides Stick together, is Don't get caught."

Cherry asks Ponyboy to come with her to get some popcorn. At the concession stand, she asks him about Johnny, and he describes to her how Johnny was jumped by the Socs. Ponyboy, Steve, and Soda were walking back from the gas station past the "wide, open field where we play football and hang out," when Steve noticed Johnny's jacket. It had a blood stain on it, and there were more stains across the grass; they then saw Johnny, "a dark motionless hump on the other side of the lot." Johnny had been beaten badly, and Ponyboy thought he might be dead. Two-bit, Darry, and Dally arrived, and Dally's reaction surprised Ponyboy: he "had seen people killed on the streets of New York's West Side. Why did he look sick now?" Johnny told them that he had been followed by a blue Mustang, and four Socs had jumped out and beaten him.

Cherry listens, and points out that "All Socs aren't like that." Ponyboy is skeptical at first, but she insists that "Things are rough all over." They go back and watch the rest of the movie with the others. Ponyboy thinks about girls in general, and how he and Johnny are both a little scared of them thanks to Two-bit's lectures.

Analysis

The theme of appearances is immediately introduced in Chapter 1. When Ponyboy becomes aware of the Socs trailing him in their car, he says, "I automatically hitched my thumbs in my jeans and slouched," to make up for his small size and appear tough.

Ponyboy describes himself to the reader as unique in the gang for loving movies and books. This characterization is demonstrated as he describes his homework - which includes reading *Great Expectations*. He relates to Pip, the main character, because "he felt marked lousy because he wasn't a gentleman or anything."

In the last paragraph of Chapter 1, the theme of dreaming is introduced indirectly. Ponyboy is falling asleep, and admits to the reader that, "I don't care about Darry. But I was still lying and I knew it. I lie to myself all the time. But I never believe me." Lying to yourself and daydreaming are equated in Ponyboy's head, suggesting that he feels guilty over his tendency to escape to alternate realities. Such flights of fancy are associated with mendacity and dishonesty; on a formal level, this is in itself intriguing, as Ponyboy serves as our perspective into the novel's world, and the reader is therefore compelled to "believe" what he says.

Hinton uses the technique of anecdote to reveal to the reader the story of Johnny's attack. Ponyboy describes it as it happened four months ago to Cherry at the concession stand. The anecdote is key to the development of Johnny's character, and the whole story, since Johnny's hatred of Socs is solidified in the attack.

The anecdote of Johnny's attack ends with a passage of foreshadowing: "They had scared him that much. He would kill the next person who jumped him." This proves true, as Johnny stabs Bob in defense of Ponyboy later. Foreshadowing is also used in the last sentence of the chapter, in which Ponyboy thinks about the Socs and says, "Man, I thought, if I had worries like that I'd consider myself lucky. I know better now."

Summary and Analysis of Chapter 3

Summary

When the movie ends, the group realizes that Cherry and Marcia don't have a way to get home, since their Soc boyfriends left them. They decide to walk to Two-bit's house, so he can get his car and drive the girls home. As they walk, Cherry and Ponyboy talk about the differences between Socs and Greasers, and how it goes beyond money. In general, Greasers are more emotional than Socs. Ponyboy notes how well he can get along with Cherry, thinking, "Nobody but Soda could really get me talking. Till I met Cherry Valance."

Ponyboy finds himself telling Cherry about Mickey Mouse, a horse that Soda loved in the stables where he used to work when he was twelve. Mickey Mouse was mean to other horses, and sometimes even to Soda, but Soda loved him like his own. Then one day Mickey Mouse got sold, and Soda had cried all night. Ponyboy, who was ten at the time, saved up his money for a year hoping to buy Mickey Mouse back for Soda. However, Ponyboy doesn't tell Cherry about the part where his brother cried.

Cherry guesses that Ponyboy reads a lot, and that he watches sunsets. Ponyboy realizes that maybe "the two different worlds we lived in weren't so different. We saw the same sunset." Suddenly, Marcia sees a blue Mustang driving toward them; it belongs to the Soc boys, Randy and Bob. Johnny is petrified, but Marcia says to "act normal," and soon the car passes by. The Socs haven't noticed them.

Cherry asks Ponyboy about Darry, and Ponyboy honestly answers that "He's hard as rock and about as human... I bet he wishes he could stick me in a home somewhere, and he'd do it, too, if Soda'd let him." Two-bit says that Ponyboy is all wrong about how Darry feels, and Johnny says he's surprised that Ponyboy feels that way, since he thought they got along. Ponyboy feels stupid because he knows he has it good compared to the home Johnny lives in, where his parents beat him up. So Ponyboy lashes out at Johnny, saying, "An' you can shut your trap, Johnny Cade, 'cause we all know you ain't wanted at home, either. And you can't blame them." Johnny winces, and Two-bit defends Johnny.

Ponyboy apologizes, but now the whole group feels down. Ponyboy cries out "It ain't fair! It ain't fair that we have all the rough breaks!" He is talking generally, about all the Greasers' situations. Two-bit smiles and says, "Like it or lump it," and the girls awkwardly remain quiet, since they don't know what to say.

Once again, the blue Mustang appears, but this time it stops beside them and Bob and Randy get out. They start defending themselves to their girlfriends, at first ignoring the Greasers. Randy refers to the guys as "bums," and Two-bit gets defensive. He breaks the end off a bottle and hands it to Ponyboy, then flips out his own switchblade. Cherry begs them not to fight, and Ponyboy makes a point of pulling her aside and assuring her that he "couldn't ever cut anyone" with the bottle Two-bit handed him. Cherry understands, but insists that she must go with the Soc boys, since "we couldn't let our parents see us with you all." Ponyboy reminds her that "some of us watch the sunset too," and she catches him off guard by replying, "I could fall in love with Dallas Winston. I hope I never see him again, or I will."

After the Mustang leaves with the Socs in it, Two-bit heads off to find a poker game; Marcia has given him her number, but he tears it up. Ponyboy and Johnny lie down in their favorite deserted lot to watch the stars, even though it is freezing cold outside and they don't have jackets. They smoke and talk vaguely about their encounter with the girls and their boyfriends. Johnny says, "I can't take much more," speaking Ponyboy's thoughts exactly. They think about a place where there are no Greasers or Socs, just "plain ordinary people."

Ponyboy begins to dream about the country, which he idealizes. In his fantasy, his parents are alive again, and Darry no longer has that "cold, hard look;" he is "like he used to be, eight months ago, before Mom and Dad were killed." Johnny comes to live with Ponyboy's family in the county, and Ponyboy's mother even convinces Dally Winston that "there was some good in the world after all." Thinking about his dream, he accidentally falls asleep. Johnny falls asleep, too.

Johnny wakes Ponyboy up suddenly, and they realize it has gotten late. Ponyboy runs home, scared of facing Darry, but Johnny stays in the lot, since his parents don't care what happens to him. When Ponyboy gets home, Darry is up waiting for him, and Soda is asleep on the sofa. Darry is "madder than I'd seen him in a long time," and he starts to yell at Ponyboy for falling asleep in the lot, saying, "Ponyboy, what on earth is the matter with you? Can't you use your head? You haven't even got a coat on." When Soda starts to stick up for Ponyboy, Darry yells at him, too. Ponyboy says, "You don't yell at him!" In response, "Darry wheeled around and slapped me so hard that it knocked me against the door." The brothers stand in silence, since nobody in their family had ever hit Ponyboy. Darry screams, "Pony, I didn't mean to!" as Ponyboy runs away, back to the lot, deciding to run away.

He finds Johnny and tells him that they are running away, and Johnny joins him without questions. When they run out of breath, they start to walk and smoke. Ponyboy tells Johnny what happened at home. Johnny confesses that he likes it better when his dad is hitting him, because at least it means he's noticing him. He feels like he has nobody in the world, whereas Ponyboy has Soda, at least. Ponyboy assures him he has the whole gang, but Johnny insists, "It ain't the same as having your own folks care about you." Now Ponyboy is cold and decides he wants to go home, but just not speak to Darry.

Analysis

Hinton uses the anecdote approach to tell the story of Soda's horse, Mickey Mouse. As Ponyboy tells the story to Cherry, the reader learns of it for the first time as well.

The telling not only demonstrates how Ponyboy feels comfortable talking to Cherry, and revealing to her a story he's never told anybody else, but characterizes Soda as capable of intense love for something that he cannot own. It is also a demonstration of Ponyboy's love for his brother: he tries to save up enough money to buy Mickey Mouse back for Soda.

Appearances, especially the Greasers' awareness of how they look around the Socs, are prominent in Chapter 3. When the Socs stop the boys with Cherry and Marcia, "Two-bit took a long drag on his cigarette, Johnny slouched and hooked his thumbs in his pockets, and I stiffened." Ponyboy notes that, "We can look meaner than anything when we want to - looking tough comes in handy."

The theme of eyes plays a big role in this chapter as well. When Ponyboy lashes out at Johnny and tells him he's not wanted at home, "Johnny's eyes went round and he winced as thought I'd belted him." Ponyboy also reads Cherry Valance's eyes, too, though: when Two-bit hands him the busted bottle to fight with, Ponyboy pulls Cherry aside to assure her he could never use it, saying, "I had to tell her that, because I'd seen her eyes when Two-bit flicked out his switch." After Darry slaps Ponyboy, Ponyboy notices that "his eyes were huge."

Ponyboy dreams of the country as he lies in the vacant lot, watching the stars with Johnny. Whenever Ponyboy feels that his situation is unbearable, he escapes by fantasizing about how things could be different. In this case, he is frustrated about being a Greaser, and wishes his parents were alive and that his whole family could escape to the country, "out of towns and away from excitement."

Hinton foreshadows the event of the burning church rescue of Chapter 6. While Ponyboy and Johnny lie in the vacant lot, Ponyboy says, "I saw Johnny's cigarette glowing in the dark and wondered vaguely what it was like inside a burning ember..." The chapter ends with another bit of foreshadowing, as Ponyboy predicts that "Things gotta get better, I figured. They couldn't get worse. I was wrong." He feels that Darry hitting him is the low point; he doesn't yet know they are about to get jumped, and that Johnny will kill Bob.

Summary and Analysis of Chapter 4

Summary

It's two-thirty in the morning, and Ponyboy and Johnny are heading home from the vacant lot, complaining about how cold it is, when they see the blue Mustang that belongs to the Socs circling the park. Five of them, including Bob and Randy, start approaching the two boys, and Ponyboy can tell they are drunk. Johnny pulls out his switchblade as they are backed against the fountain. Ponyboy and Johnny are both terrified, but they try to look tough.

The Socs start taunting them, calling them "White trash with long hair," and Ponyboy responds by spitting at them. Bob tells Ponyboy, "You could use a bath, greaser," and tells David, another Soc, to "give the kid a bath." David grabs Ponyboy and holds his head under the water of the fountain. Just as Ponyboy thinks he's about to die, he wakes up on the pavement next to the fountain, "coughing water and gasping."

Johnny is sitting next to him, and next to them lies the body of Bob, in a pool of blood. Ponyboy sees that Johnny has killed him with the switchblade, and vomits. Johnny tells him that the other Socs ran away when he stabbed Bob. Ponyboy starts to panic, screaming, "What are we gonna do?" and Johnny tries to calm him down, deciding they'll need money, a gun, and a plan. They decide to find Dally and ask him for help.

They go to Buck Merril's house to find Dally, because they remember there is a party there that Dally said he was going to. Buck answers the door, clearly drunk, but goes to get Dally when the boys ask for him. Dally appears in the doorway, pretty sober, and listens to what happened. Dally has been in a fight with Tim Shepard, and has "cracked some ribs." He lets them inside when he sees that they are cold and wet, and gives them fifty dollars and a loaded gun. He also gives Ponyboy one of Buck's shirts and his own brown leather jacket. He gives them instructions to get on a freight train to Windrixville, then find an abandoned church on top of Jay Mountain.

The boys sneak into an open boxcar on the train, avoiding being caught by one of the railroad workers. It hits Ponyboy for the first time that they are in real trouble, that Johnny has murdered someone and now they are running away. They are exhausted, and Ponyboy falls asleep.

The boys jump off the train at Windrixville, and Ponyboy is barely awake. He realizes they are in the country, and vaguely remembers his daydream about how wonderful the country is. They want to get to Jay Mountain, but don't know where to go. They want to ask someone, but Ponyboy realizes they look nothing like farm boys, and is afraid people will judge them, thinking "They'll know we're hoods the minute they see us." Johnny's legs are still asleep from Ponyboy leaning on them as he slept, so he tells Ponyboy to "quit slouching like a thug" and go ask someone for directions.

As Ponyboy walks off, he thinks about how Darry and Sodapop will react when he doesn't come home. He can't believe it was only the night before that he met Cherry Valance at the drive-in. He worries about being on the run forever, and maybe being sent to a reformatory. He runs into a farmer driving a tractor, and politely asks where Jay Mountain is, lying and saying that they are playing army and he is supposed to "report to headquarters there." He scares himself because it's so easy for him to lie.

The boys climb up to the church, feeling beyond exhausted. Ponyboy remembers how he used to go to church all the time, but one Sunday he talked Soda and Johnny into going with him. The whole gang showed up, and embarrassed Ponyboy by acting up and drawing attention to themselves. Now Ponyboy and Johnny flop down on the floor of the church and fall asleep immediately.

Analysis

One of the distinguishing characteristics of Hinton's prose is its effort to faithfully replicate a certain way of speaking and writing among "tough" youths. Ponyboy's role as narrator casts the proceedings and colors the language; what emerges is a specific vernacular. At points, his narration borders on stream of consciousness. In this chapter, the repetition of certain lines lends the reader the impression of drifting inside Ponyboy's head. For example, after Ponyboy realizes Johnny has killed Bob, Hinton writes (or Ponyboy thinks): "This can't be happening. This can't be happening. This can't be..." He is dizzy, so the thought trails off.

Eyes are prominent in this chapter, and especially Johnny's. As the five Soc boys approach him and Ponyboy, "his eyes were wild-looking, like the eyes of an animal in a trap." After Bob calls the boys "White trash with long hair," Ponyboy notices that Johnny's "eyes were smoldering." When Ponyboy comes to after almost being drowned, he notes Johnny's expression, fresh from Bob's kill: "his eyes were huger than I'd ever seen them."

The theme of appearances comes into play when the Socs approach Johnny and Ponyboy: the two young boys try to look tough. "Johnny had a blank, tough look on his face - you'd have had to know him to see the panic in his eyes. I stared at the Socs coolly. Maybe they could scare us to death, but we'd never let them have the satisfaction of knowing." Later, when the boys are going to ask for directions to Jay Mountain, Ponyboy sees Johnny "as a stranger might see him," and realizes that they will never pass for farm boys. He thinks, "They'll know we're hoods the minute they see us."

Dreaming of the country segues into a disappointing reality when the boys jump off the train in Windrixville. Ponyboy notices that "the clouds were pink and meadowlarks were singing," and thinks to himself that finally he has arrived in the country. But later, as he looks for someone to ask directions, he thinks to himself, "I was in the country, but I knew I wasn't going to like it as much as I'd thought I would."

Linked to the theme of dreaming of the country is that of pretending, which Ponyboy does to escape situations he can't deal with. The line between "pretending" and "lying" is blurred; both come easily to Ponyboy. "I can lie so easily that it spooks me sometimes," he concedes. It's both a boast and a confession, and, indeed, a sense of guilt permeates his descriptions of his own dreams and his own ruses.

The end of the chapter includes a bit of foreshadowing, when Ponyboy says that "this church gave me a kind of creepy feeling. What do you call it? Premonition?" Here, with these questions, Hinton uses the technique of direct address, when the narrator speaks to the reader personally. The foreshadowing is self-conscious, since Ponyboy makes a point of calling it a premonition.

Summary and Analysis of Chapter 5

Summary

Ponyboy wakes up in the abandoned church, and at first thinks he has dreamed everything that has happened. He pretends for a moment that he is back home, and it is a usual weekend morning. When he gives up pretending, he realizes that Johnny is gone, and has left a note in the dust on the floor that he's gone to get supplies.

Ponyboy wanders outside to get a drink from the pump behind the church. He feels overwhelmed, and can't keep track of how much time has passed since the night before. Johnny returns, and Ponyboy is so glad to see him that he trips and falls down the steps. They go inside the church, and Johnny reveals that he's bought food (including a week's supply of baloney) and a copy of *Gone with the Wind* for Ponyboy, since he remembered that Ponyboy had wanted to read it.

Johnny has bought peroxide, and reveals his plan to cut their hair and bleach Ponyboy's, as a disguise. Ponyboy is horrified, since he is proud of his hair. After it's all done, Ponyboy looks at himself in the mirror and thinks that he looks "younger and scareder," not at all like himself. Then Johnny washes the grease out of his hair, and Ponyboy cuts it off. Ponyboy sulks about losing his hair, but Johnny is optimistic, saying "It's just hair."

The boys talk about the little store that Johnny bought the goods from, and how Two-bit would have stolen everything easily from it because the products were just lying out. Thinking about Two-bit makes them homesick for the gang, though, and when Ponyboy starts talking about the night before, Johnny tells him, "Stop it!" and begins to cry. Ponyboy comforts him, but starts to cry himself. Soon they fall asleep, and when they wake up, they decide they're "all cried out now," and that they can "take whatever was coming now."

Over the next four or five days, Ponyboy and Johnny kill time by playing cards and reading *Gone with the Wind*. Johnny becomes interested in the idea of gallant southern gentlemen, and says he thinks that Dally is most like them. Ponyboy is shocked, but realizes for the first time "the extent of Johnny's hero-worship for Dally Winston." They stay in the back of the church so they won't be seen by the rare passers-by.

One morning, Ponyboy wakes up early and goes to sit outside and have a smoke. He watches the sunrise, and soon Johnny joins him, commenting on the beauty of the sunrise and saying it's "too bad it couldn't stay like that all the time." That reminds Ponyboy of the poem "Nothing Gold Can Stay" by Robert Frost, and he recites it for Johnny. They are both baffled by the poem, and Ponyboy admits that "I never quite got what he meant by it." Johnny brings up Ponyboy's family, and they decide that the two of them are different from the rest of the gang.

On the fifth day, Ponyboy is sick of eating baloney and also sick from smoking so much, and just as he curls up to fall asleep, he hears a whistle. It is Dally, and Ponyboy sees him as representing "one thing: contact with the outside world." He hands Ponyboy a letter from Sodapop, who suspected that Dally knew where the boys were hiding, and asked him to bring the letter to Ponyboy. It says that Darry feels terrible for the events of the night the boys ran away.

Dally tells them how he was brought into the police station because "I get hauled in for everything that happens in our turf," and how he misled the police into thinking the boys ran off to Texas. He teases Ponyboy for his new haircut and color. Then they get in the car and drive to Dairy Queen, where they "gorged on barbecue sandwiches and banana splits," since they have been starving and are tired of an all-baloney diet.

Dally updates them that the Socs are "having all-out warfare all over the city," since Bob had a lot of friends and now they want revenge on the Greasers. Dally has started carrying a gun, although he says it's not loaded. He also tells them that Cherry Valance is spying for them.

Analysis

Ponyboy continues pretending, in the beginning of this chapter, to deal with the frightening situation in which he finds himself. When he doesn't recognize his surroundings upon waking, he imagines that he is home in bed, and that his brothers have already woken up. In his fantasy, they eat breakfast and then go outside and play football.

Cutting and dying their hair is an important change for the boys, especially for Ponyboy, who has purposefully grown his hair long like Soda's. When Johnny reveals his plan to cut it, Ponyboy narrates, "It was my pride... Our hair labeled us greasers, too - it was our trademark. The one thing we were proud of. Maybe we couldn't have Corvairs or madras shirts, but we could have hair." Cutting it off causes a kind of identity crisis, a Samson-like transformation.

Gone with the Wind is also introduced in this chapter, as an important indicator of the two boys' different outlooks. They are both interested in the idea of the gallant southern gentleman, but have different ideas of who of their gang is the most gallant. Johnny thinks it is Dally, but Ponyboy thinks of Soda, Two-bit, and even Darry as having more "superman qualities."

The poem "Nothing Gold Can Stay" serves as a reflection on the boys' lives, although Ponyboy admits that the meaning eludes him. We as readers can understand the melancholy message that their youth is gold, but is passing; Johnny's life is gold, but will pass by the end of the story.

Tied to the poem "Nothing Gold Can Stay" is the theme of sunsets, which reappears in this chapter as representing the intangible thing that makes Ponyboy, Johnny, and Cherry Valance "different." Johnny confesses that he never noticed "colors and clouds and stuff" until Ponyboy pointed them out to him. The fact that Ponyboy cannot see the sunset from the back of the church represents how disconnected he feels from reality and his own identity. In this sense, sunsets separate, whereas in other parts of the novel they connect; Hinton thereby hints at how we might imbue everyday occurrences and objects with our own hopes, wishes, and emotions. Like that other great expressionist of youthful rebellion, filmmaker Nicholas Ray, Hinton posits a world colored by the dreams of its under-age inhabitants.

Summary and Analysis of Chapter 6

Summary

Ponyboy and Johnny react with surprise to the fact that Cherry Valance has been acting as a spy for the Greasers. Dally explains that Cherry approached the Greasers in the vacant lot and said that she felt guilty for the whole mess, and that she "would testify that the Socs were drunk and looking for a fight and that you fought back in self-defense." He says that it's pretty apparent Cherry hates him, but Ponyboy knows it's because she's afraid of falling for him that she acts so cold.

After they chat a little bit about the church and the country, Johnny announces that they are turning themselves in. He explains that he has no record, so he has a good chance of "bein' let off easy," and that he won't say Dally helped them at all. He thinks it's unfair for Ponyboy to have to hide away with him. Then he asks Dally, "I don't guess my parents are worried about me or anything?" Dally replies that they haven't asked about him, and it is clear this news depresses Johnny, even though he doesn't say anything. As they drive back to the church, Ponyboy thinks about how even though the gang is very close, it can't take the place of parents or real family.

Dally seems angry as they drive back, and Johnny and Ponyboy think it's because he is annoyed they didn't turn themselves in earlier, if at all, to save him trouble. But he explains "in a pleading, high voice" that he just doesn't want Johnny to get hardened in jail. Ponyboy realizes how tenderly Dally feels for Johnny, and thinks about what Dally might have been like before he was toughened on the streets and in jail.

When the arrive at the church, they see it is on fire. Ponyboy hops out of the car right away, although Dally wants him to get back in so they can leave. They approach a man who turns out to be Jerry Wood, a teacher who was having a picnic with schoolchildren when the church caught on fire. Ponyboy and Johnny assume they started the fire with a cigarette accidentally. Then Mrs. O'Brient, another schoolteacher, runs up and says that some of the children are missing. They all hear yelling from inside the church, and realize that some of the children must be trapped.

Ponyboy runs toward the church, throws a rock through a window, and pulls himself inside. He realizes that Johnny has followed him, but that Jerry Wood was too fat to get through the window. They run to the back of the church, and find a group of children "about eight years old or younger, huddled in a corner." Johnny takes charge and starts tossing the kids out the nearest window. Ponyboy starts to help. As the roof starts to crumble, Johnny shoves Ponyboy out of the window ahead of himself. Ponyboy hears Johnny scream, and then Dally whacks him on the back and he "went down into a peaceful darkness."

Ponyboy wakes up in an ambulance, bewildered. Jerry Wood is with him, and explains that Dally hit him so hard because the back of his jacket was on fire. When

Ponyboy asks him about Dally and Johnny, Jerry says that Dally has burned one of his arms badly, but that he will be all right, but he is unsure about Johnny, since he might have a broken back from the collapsing roof. He asks if they were "sent straight from Heaven," and Ponyboy explains that they are "Greasers. You know, like hoods, JD's." Jerry is shocked when Ponyboy tells him Johnny is wanted for murder, but says they are going to the hospital, not the police station.

In the waiting room, Ponyboy smokes a cigarette and Jerry reprimands him for being too young to smoke. Soda and Darry come to see him; Soda bemoans the loss of his "tuff, tuff hair," but Darry looks at him with "pleading" eyes. Ponyboy realizes he is crying, and that he hasn't seen him cry in years. Ponyboy understands how much Darry cares about him, and that maybe the reason he is so strict is because he wants to keep him safe.

Analysis

Cherry Valance helps the Greasers, and thereby creates a bridge of non-violence between the two rival gangs. Ponyboy recognizes that "it wasn't Cherry the Soc who was helping us, it was Cherry the dreamer who watched sunsets and couldn't stand fights." Ponyboy begins to understand that Cherry and he have something in common outside their respective social statuses.

Our understanding of Johnny's character is deepened by his conversation with Dally, in which he asks, trying not to appear eager, "I don't guess my parents are worried about me or anything?" Dally has to answer that his parents haven't asked about him. That his parents don't care about him even when he is wanted for murder and has disappeared explains Johnny's outward meekness -- but it also hints at his inner strength and independence. He is cut off.

The relationship between Dally and Johnny grows stronger in this chapter, and it becomes clear that, while Johnny feels hero-worship toward Dally, Dally wants to protect Johnny and keep him from turning out the way he himself has. As they drive back to the church, he explains, "You get hardened in jail. I don't want that to happen to you. Like it happened to me..." His emotional outburst makes Ponyboy think of him before he was hardened and tough, and reflect on how he came to be that way.

As Ponyboy charges into the school, he "remembered wondering what it was like in a burning ember, and I thought: Now I know, it's a red hell." The burning of the church has of course been foreshadowed (when the boys lay in the vacant lot watching the stars and Ponyboy looked at Johnny's cigarette end, wondering what it was like inside a burning ember.)

Johnny's eyes, a running theme throughout the novel, change dramatically in this chapter as he acts heroically. Ponyboy notes that "that was the only time I can think of when I saw him without that defeated, suspicious look in his eyes." Even at the beginning of the chapter, "his big black eyes grew bigger than ever" at the thought of going to jail, since he was afraid of the police; now, he is confident and acting like a hero, and the change is reflected in his eyes. Once again, Hinton uses concrete physical details and splashes of corporeality to suggest the inner workings of her characters; it's a kind of skin-level expressionism at play, reflecting as it does an adolescent's dawning awareness of the world around him - a world in which eyes are windows to the soul, haircuts and dress styles determine a boy's place in society, and entire relationships are refracted through lingo.

At the end of the chapter, when Soda and Darry come to the hospital, Ponyboy has a revelation about his relationship with Darry. He sees his oldest brother cry for the first time in years. It occurs to him that "Darry did care about me, maybe as much as he cared about Soda, and because he cared he was trying too hard to make something of me." Darry is terrified of losing another person he loves, and Ponyboy wonders "how I could ever have thought him hard and unfeeling."

Summary and Analysis of Chapters 7 and 8

Summary

Ponyboy sits in the waiting room with Darry and Soda, who is entertaining the reporters and policemen by acting silly. Jerry Wood tells Ponyboy that the reporters wouldn't have been taking so many pictures if his older brothers weren't so handsome. But soon the boys become tired, and Soda lies down to fall asleep. Darry tells Ponyboy that Soda hardly slept all week, and Soda says the same is true for Darry.

After Darry convinces a doctor that "we were about as much family as Dally and Johnny had," they learn that Dally will be okay, though one of his arms will always have burn scars. Johnny, on the other hand, is in critical condition with a broken back and third-degree burns. Even if he survives, he will be crippled. None of the brothers cry, but they are all stunned into silence. They decide to drive home, and Ponyboy falls asleep on the way. Darry carries him inside and puts him in bed.

The next morning, Ponyboy wakes up before Darry or Soda and takes a shower. He makes eggs and chocolate cake for breakfast; all of them like to eat it for breakfast, and can do so whenever they want with no parents. Two-Bit and Steve come in without knocking, as is their custom, and Ponyboy explains to the reader that all the gang know they can come over and stay at his house whenever they want, or need somewhere to sleep, since the door is never locked.

Two-Bit scoops Ponyboy up and spins him around, because he's missed him, and sends one of the eggs Ponyboy is preparing flying; Ponyboy accidentally crushes the other egg in his hand, and scolds Two-Bit for ruining breakfast. Two-Bit and Steve tease him good-naturedly for his haircut, and Steve shows him the newspaper, with the headline "Juvenile Delinquents Turn Heroes." There are many stories about the boys in the paper, covering the murder, the church burning, and all the surrounding events. Both Cherry and Randy Adderson have said in interviews that the Socs were drunk during the fight, and that Johnny had killed Bob in self-defense.

One article is all about Darry, Soda, and Ponyboy living on their own, and it says that they shouldn't be separated. This makes Ponyboy realize that there is a chance they *might* be, and that he might be put in a "boy's home" after he appears in juvenile court for running away. Ponyboy balks at this news, even though Steve tells him not to worry about it. Darry and Soda come into the kitchen, and Ponyboy asks Darry if he knew about the juvenile court appearance; Darry says he did.

Then Ponyboy tells Darry that he had "one of those dreams last night. The one I can't ever remember." He had the same dream the night of his parents' funeral, and "woke up screaming bloody murder" but unable to remember what it was about. The dream started reoccurring, so Soda started sleeping with Ponyboy. Two-Bit asks him if it was very bad, but Ponyboy lies and says it wasn't.

Sodapop and Steve start a conversation about how they'll throw a party once they beat the Socs for good, and Ponyboy makes the mistake of asking about Sandy. He finds out that Sandy went to live with her grandmother in Florida, since her parents didn't want her to marry Soda. There is an awkward moment, and Ponyboy realizes how upset Soda must be.

Darry, Soda, and Steve have to head to work, and Two-Bit offers to "baby-sit" Ponyboy, since Darry doesn't want to leave him alone. Two-Bit and Ponyboy immediately start wrestling, and Darry tells Two-Bit to "lay off." The other boys leave, and as Ponyboy does the dishes, Two-Bit tells him about "one of his many exploits." They clean up the house for the reporters, then leave.

They walk to Tasty Freeze to get Cokes, and the blue Mustang "that had been trailing us for eight blocks" pulls in behind them. Randy Adderson gets out, and Ponyboy recognizes him. Two-Bit warns Randy, "You know the rules. No jazz before the rumble," but Randy says he just wants to talk to Ponyboy. Ponyboy gets in the car with him, and Randy asks him how he had the guts to save the kids from the burning church. Then he confesses that he's not going to show up to the planned rumble that night.

Ponyboy looks at Randy and realizes that "he was seventeen or so, but he was already old," like Dally. Randy tells Ponyboy that Bob's mother has had a nervous breakdown after her son's death, and explains how Bob was so spoiled that all he wanted was for someone to tell him "No," or to get in trouble with his parents, but it never happened. Then he asks about Johnny. He says he's sick of all the fighting, and instead of going to the rumble, he's going to leave town. Ponyboy gets out of the car, saying, "You would have saved those kids if you had been there. You'd have saved them the same as we did." He goes back to Two-Bit, and decides that "Things were rough all over, but it was better that way. That way you could tell the other guy was human too."

As Chapter 8 begins, Ponyboy and Two-Bit arrive at the hospital, but the nurses tell them Johnny cannot have any visitors. Finally, one of the doctors tells he nurses to let them go in, since Johnny has been asking for them. From the tone the doctor uses, Ponyboy can tell that Johnny really is dying. When they go into the room, Johnny tries to smile. Two-Bit tells him about the rumble that's going to happen that night, and they talk about how Johnny is in the paper for being a hero. Johnny asks for another copy of *Gone with the Wind,* and Two-Bit runs down to the drugstore to buy one.

When Johnny and Ponyboy are alone, Johnny asks, "I'm pretty bad off, ain't I, Pony?" and Ponyboy tries to reassure him that he'll be okay. Johnny says that he knows he won't be able to walk again, and confesses that he's scared. He doesn't want to die at only sixteen years old. Ponyboy continues to try to reassure him.

Then a nurse comes in and says that Johnny's mother is there to see him, but Johnny says firmly, "I don't want to see her." He says to tell his mother "For once just to leave me alone," then he passes out from exertion. The nurse tells Ponyboy he has to leave, and turns Two-Bit away as he arrives with the copy of *Gone with the Wind.* As they walk back down the hospital hall, they see Johnny's mother complaining that she's not allowed to see him. When she sees them, she tells them it is their fault that Johnny was hurt. They feel terrible that Johnny has to "live with that," and Ponyboy hopes that the nurse will do what Johnny wants and not let his mother in to see him.

Ponyboy and Two-Bit go into Dally's room next. He tells them that Tim Shepard has come by to see him, and Ponyboy ponders how they can be such close friends and beat each other up all the time. Dally asks how Johnny is doing, and "swore between clenched teeth" when Two-Bit says he's not doing well. Dally asks for Two-Bit's "black-handled switch," and Two-Bit gives it to him. Even though Two-Bit has stolen it and is very proud of it, he gives it up to Dally "without a moment's hesitation." Dally has determined to go to the rumble, and they don't argue.

Ponyboy and Two-Bit take the bus home, but Ponyboy almost falls asleep on the bench waiting for it. He feels sick, but asks Two-Bit not to tell Darry because he wants to fight that night. Two-Bit points out that "The only thing that keeps Darry from bein' a Soc is us." Ponyboy has known this for a long time, and regrets it. Ponyboy has a bad premonition about the rumble that night, but Two-Bit tells him to brush it off.

When they get to the vacant lot, Cherry is there in her Corvette. She reports that the Socs are going to "play your way. No weapons, fair deal. Your rules." When Two-Bit leaves, Cherry asks Ponyboy to stay behind for a minute. She tells him Randy isn't going to the rumble, but he says he already knows. She explains that he's really upset after Bob's death, and Ponyboy thinks about how upset Soda or Steve would be if the other one was killed.

She asks about Johnny, but says she can't bring herself to go visit him in the hospital because he is the one who killed her boyfriend, Bob. Ponyboy understands, but is still mad because he knows that it's not Johnny's fault Bob is dead. He tells her, "I wouldn't want you to see him. You're a traitor to your own kind and not loyal to us." He notices that she is about to cry, and feels ashamed. She says she wasn't trying to give him charity, she just liked him from the start. Ponyboy makes amends by asking, "can you see the sunset real good from the West Side?" she is surprised, but answers yes. He says, "You can see it good from the East Side, too," once again closing the gap between them. Then he walks home.

Analysis

Once again, Ponyboy has a difficult situation to deal with, and he does so by escaping into dreams, by pretending the situation is different. After hearing the news that, should Johnny live he will be crippled for the rest of his life, Ponyboy tells himself, "I'm dreaming. I'll wake up at home or in the church and everything'll be like it used to be." But he has to admit that "I didn't believe myself." He finds it impossible to convince himself of an alternate truth, although by the next chapter he will have almost completely convinced himself of it.

In Chapter 7, Randy becomes one of the people who appreciate sunsets. Ponyboy realizes, "Cherry had said her friends were too cool to feel anything, and yet she could remember watching sunsets. Randy was supposed to be too cool to feel anything, and yet there was pain in his eyes." As he tells Ponyboy that he is tired of fighting and is going to leave town instead of going to the rumble, Ponyboy remembers Cherry saying "Things are rough all over," and understands what she meant. It is evident that Ponyboy makes the link between Randy, as more than a Soc, and himself, as more than a Greaser, when he says, "You would have saved those kids if you had been there. You'd have saved them the same as we did."

Eyes continue to be an important indicator of personality in these chapters. When Randy talks to Ponyboy in the car, Ponyboy recognizes "pain in his eyes." Ponyboy also points out the difference between Johnny and his mother as reflected in their eyes: "Johnnycake's eyes were fearful and sensitive; hers were cheap and hard." The last thing Ponyboy notes in the chapter is Cherry Valance's eyes, saying, "She had green eyes."

In Chapter 8, the gap between Socs and Greasers is bridged for Ponyboy yet again, this time because of the connection he sees between Bob and Randy's relationship and that of Soda and Steve. Cherry explains how upset Randy is after Bob's death, and Ponyboy thinks, "What if one of them saw the other killed? Would that make them stop fighting? No, I thought, maybe it would make Soda stop, but not Steve. He'd go on hating and fighting. Maybe that was what Bob would have done if it had been Randy instead of him."

Foreshadowing reappears in Chapter 8, and Ponyboy is conscious of it as a character as well as as the narrator. As he and Two-bit ride the bus home, he thinks, "I had a sick feeling in my stomach and it wasn't from being ill. It was the same kind of helplessness I'd felt that night Darry yelled at me for going to sleep in the lot. I had the same deathly fear that something was going to happen that none of us could stop. As we got off the bus I finally said it. 'Tonight - I don't like it one bit.'" Ponyboy's stance as narrator looking back on the past melds with his stance within his own story - that is, as protagonist. It is as though the purely literary use of foreshadowing here takes on a greater significance, and as though Ponyboy changes the past by observing it. The echoes of impending doom are pure pulp, but they complicate Ponyboy's role as both storyteller and participant, blurring the line between the two.

Summary and Analysis of Chapter 9

Summary

Ponyboy gets back to his house at almost six-thirty, late for supper. He can hardly eat because he doesn't feel well, and he sneaks some aspirins when his brothers aren't looking. Then he takes a shower to get "spruced up" before the rumble, like he and Soda always do. He, Soda, and Steve use more hair grease than they need to, to maintain their image of toughness.

While they wait for Two-Bit to show up, Ponyboy asks the others if they like fighting and why. Soda says he does, because "It's action. It's a contest. Like a drag race or a dance or something." Steve's answer is because "I want to beat those Socs' heads in. When I get in a fight I want to stomp the other guy good. I like it, too." Darry doesn't answer, just gives Ponyboy "one of those looks that hide what he's thinking." But Soda chimes in that Darry likes to show off his muscles, and Ponyboy thinks that's true. Since everyone else likes fighting, Ponyboy feels out of place.

Darry tells him he thinks it's not a good idea for him to go to the fight, since he's "tensed up too much." But Soda says to let Ponyboy come, since there are no weapons. None of the other smaller guys will be there; not Johnny or Dally or Curly Shepard, Tim Shepard's little brother, because he's in the reformatory. Finally Darry gives in and says he'll let Ponyboy fight.

The boys start getting pumped up for the rumble, doing acrobatics and shouting as they leave the house. They do a role play in which Darry and Two-Bit pretend to be snobby Socs, saying "Get thee hence, white trash," while Soda embraces the Greaser stereotypes, chanting, "I blacken the name of our fair city." Ponyboy asks Two-Bit why he likes to fight, and he responds, "Shoot, everybody fights." Ponyboy realizes that each member of the gang fights for a different reason: Soda for fun, Steve for hatred, Darry for pride, and Two-Bit for conformity... but Ponyboy doesn't know why he himself fights. Darry reminds Ponyboy and Soda to run away if the police show up, so they don't get put in a boys' home.

When the gang gets to the vacant lot, Tim Shepard and his gang are already there. Ponyboy notes that the difference between their gang and the Shepard gang is that Tim Shepard uses "strict discipline;" there is a clear leader and they are organized, while Ponyboy's gang is "just buddies who stuck together." There's also another Greaser gang from Brumly, a suburb. They all shake hands to prove that their on the same side in the rumble. When Tim Shepard reaches Ponyboy, he asks about how he and Johnny killed the Soc; Ponyboy pretends to be proud of it. He also notices he's the youngest one there, since Curly Shepard is in the reformatory for breaking into a liquor store.

One of the guys from the Brumly gang asks Ponyboy about Darry, saying he looks like a good rumbler. Ponyboy looks around at the other members of his gang and realizes that since they're not using weapons, Darry really is the best equipped for the fight. But when Tim Shepard calls Darry over, Ponyboy thinks "He shouldn't be here." None of their gang should be there, because "We're greasers, but not hoods, and we don't belong with this bunch of future convicts."

The Socs start arriving at the vacant lot; there are twenty-two Socs and twenty Greasers. Ponyboy notices how the Socs don't look like they're going to a rumble at all, and decides that since "people usually go by looks," it makes sense that the Greasers always get in trouble. One of the Socs clarifies the rules, that "the first to run lose," and that they won't use weapons.

Then Darry steps foward to start the rumble off, saying that he'll take on any of the Socs. Paul Holden steps forward from the Soc side; he is one of Darry's ex-friends from high school, and now he looks at Darry with a mixture of contempt, pity, and hate. Ponyboy realizes that Darry is not only jealous of Paul and the opportunities he has that Darry doesn't, but he is ashamed to be representing the Greasers. The two young men start to circle each other in the silence, and Ponyboy thinks about how they shouldn't hate each other.

Then Dally runs to join them, yelling "Hold up!" When Darry looks up to see who yelled, Paul punches him in the jaw and the rumble begins. As Ponyboy fights alongside Dally, Dally explains that he escaped the hospital by threatening a nurse with Two-Bit's switchblade. Darry is protecting Ponyboy, and Ponyboy decides to help Dally since one of his arms is unusable. But one of the Socs kicks Ponyboy in the head so hard he feels like he's about to black out.

Soon, the Socs run away, and Darry announces that the Greasers have won the rumble. Immediately, Dally grabs Ponyboy and says they're going to see Johnny, since he's getting worse and wants to see Ponyboy. Dally is speeding on the way to the hospital and gets pulled over, but since Ponyboy looks sick, he lies and says that they are going there to get Ponyboy treated. The cop offers to escort them the rest of the way to the hospital.

Dally begins "raving on and on" about how he wishes Johnny had been tougher, like himself, so he wouldn't have gotten into this mess. Ponyboy doesn't understand the rest, because he's too sick. When they run inside the hospital and reach Johnny's room, the doctor says, "I'm sorry boys, but he's dying." But Dally insists that they have to see him, threatening the doctor with a knife.

Johnny looks terrible, and Ponyboy worries that he's already dead. Dally tells Johnny how they won the rumble, but Johnny mumbles "Useless... fighting's no good..." Dally tells him that he is proud of him, and "Johnny's eyes glowed," because Dally is his hero. Then he asks for Ponyboy, and whispers, "Stay gold, Ponyboy. Stay gold..." before dying. Ponyboy notes that he doesn't look peaceful, he just looks dead.

Dally pushes Johnny's hair back, and says, "That's what you get for tryin' to help people, you little punk, that's what you get..." Then he slams himself into the wall, punching it and saying, "Damnit, Johnny, please don't die." Then he runs out of the room and down the hall.

Analysis

Soda launches the role playing game with the proclamation: "I am a greaser. I am a JD and a hood. I blacken the name of our fair city. I beat up people. I rob gas stations. I am a menace to society. Man, do I have fun!" It's a blast of verbal swagger, machismo through words, and it allows the boys to get excited about their rumble. At the same time, however, it suggests just how conscious they are of their appearance in the eyes of the rest of society. They embrace the stereotypes that cast them, as though by adopting them they might rise above them. In this sense they suggest nothing so much as kids playing at being gangsters or gunslingers; it's all theater, all role-playing - until someone gets hurt, that is.

When the Socs arrive at the rumble, Ponyboy reflects on the falsity of appearances. He realizes that the reason the Socs never get blamed for causing trouble is because "We look hoody and they look decent." Although most of the Greasers are "pretty decent guys underneath all that grease," and the Socs are "just cold-blooded mean," it doesn't matter because "people usually go by looks."

The confrontation between Darry and Paul Holden serves to demonstrate the divide between the Greasers and the Socs - a divide that runs deeper than appearances. Ponyboy sees that "something flickered behind Darry's eyes and then they were ice again," when Paul says, "Hello, Darrel." Ponyboy knows that while Paul looks at Darry with a mixture of contempt, pity, and hate, Darry is jealous of Paul and ashamed to represent the Greasers. Although they both played football together in high school, Paul is in college and Darry is working, unable to afford school; the vicissitudes of life have separated them.

Before he dies, Johnny whispers to Ponyboy, "Stay gold, Ponyboy. Stay gold..." He is referencing the poem by Robert Frost that Ponyboy recited aloud when they were sitting on the back porch of the church, watching the sunrise. By dying, Johnny is fulfilling the prophecy of the poem that "Nothing gold can stay." But he hopes for Ponyboy to fulfill his own potential and not wind up like him.

Dally's reaction to Johnny's death is a great show of emotion for someone who Ponyboy thinks is always cool. Clearly, Dally loves Johnny, and cannot handle the pain that accompanies his death. However, he left Johnny in the hospital to attend the rumble, even though he knew Johnny was dying. Although he loves Johnny, he cannot separate himself from the violence that is part of his personality, and he expresses his frustration by fighting Socs. It's a lose-lose, and it is here that Hinton's narrative suggests the fatalism of tragedy.

Summary and Analysis of Chapters 10 and 11

Summary

Since Dally has left in the car, Ponyboy walks home from the hospital by himself, pretending that Johnny isn't really dead. He ends up wandering around "in a stupor" until a man in his mid-twenties asks him if he needs a ride. The man points out that Ponyboy is bleeding, and Ponyboy discovers that his head is injured.

When he is dropped off at his house, Ponyboy finds the remainder of the gang in the living room, tending their wounds from the rumble. When Darry asks where he has been, Ponyboy has to break the news that Johnny has died. The gang responds with "stricken silence." He also reports that Dallas has run off, since he couldn't take it. Ponyboy starts shaking; his heart is beating loudly and he feels as if he will fall over. Then Dally calls from a payphone, saying he's just robbed a grocery store and is running from the cops. As the gang rushes out of the house, Ponyboy feels as if he is about to faint.

They arrive at the vacant lot just as Dally does, from the opposite direction. The police pull up in their cars and jump out. Dally pulls his gun out and raises it; the policemen fire at him, killing him. Ponyboy realizes that Dally had wanted them to kill him. Dally has died "violent and young and desperate," but "he died gallant." Then Ponyboy does pass out.

When Ponyboy wakes up, the house is disconcertingly silent, and Soda is sitting next to him on the bed. Soda tells him that he is sick, and should go back to sleep. Ponyboy asks, "Is Darry sorry I'm sick?" and Soda is confused by the question, but responds that yes, Darry is sorry. Then Ponyboy falls back asleep. When Ponyboy comes to again, he sees Darry asleep in the armchair next to his bed. Darry tells him he's been very sick with exhaustion, shock, and a minor concussion. Suddenly Ponyboy remembers that Johnny and Dally are dead. But he tells himself, "Don't remember. Don't remember." Darry tells him that he has been "asleep and delirious" for over three days. Ponyboy begins to worry about having to go to court, and asks Darry if they will get split up, but Darry doesn't know.

Darry says that Ponyboy has been in the hospital, asking for him and Soda and their parents. Ponyboy worries that maybe, in his delirious state, he hasn't been asking for Darry at all, but he doesn't remember, and doesn't ask Darry. Johnny has left Ponyboy his copy of *Gone with the Wind*, but Ponyboy doesn't want to finish it since he'd "never get past the part where the Southern gentlemen go riding into sure death because they are gallant."

Ponyboy asks for Soda, but scolds himself for not being comfortable to talk to Darry. Soda immediately bounds into the room, although Darry has said he's exhausted and can hardly stay awake. Darry goes to make Ponyboy some mushroom soup, leaving the two younger brothers together. Ponyboy asks Soda what he said while he was delirious, and Soda responds that mostly he thought he was in Windrixville, and that he wouldn't eat anything because he kept saying he didn't like baloney. Ponyboy asks Soda if he really asked for Darry, since he is worried that maybe he didn't, but Soda confirms that he did. Then Soda gets into bed with him and they both fall asleep before Darry returns with the soup.

As Chapter 11 begins, Ponyboy has been in bed for a week more. He flips through one of Soda's old yearbooks and finds Bob Sheldon, and for the first time wonders what Bob is really like. He remembers that Cherry Valance loved Bob, and tries to understand the person she knew: "a reckless, hot-tempered boy, cocky and scared stiff at the same time."

Darry comes in and says that a guy named Randy is there to see Ponyboy. Although Ponyboy has been embarrassed when school friends came by to visit, since their house is run-down, he doesn't much care what Randy thinks. Randy comes into the bedroom, and wants to talk about how they have to go to court the next day. Ponyboy feels resentful of Randy for acting like he is "mixed up in all this," when things will no doubt turn out fine for him, since "his old man was rich." He also resents being made to think about the pending hearing, since he's been putting off thinking about it. Ponyboy explains to Randy that he is worried that the judge might send him and Soda to a boys' home. He notices that Randy looks sincerely worried about that possibility, and thinks it's strange.

When Randy mentions how Johnny killed Bob, it becomes clear that Ponyboy is in denial about the events of the past weeks. He says that he was the one who killed Bob, and that Johnny is not dead. Then Darry tells Randy he should leave, and Ponyboy overhears him saying that "he's still pretty racked up mentally and emotionally." Ponyboy doesn't register what this means, though, and instead resents Randy for implying that Johnny was involved in Bob's death. Darry scolds Ponyboy for smoking in bed and keeping his room messy, calling him "little buddy;" it's the first time he's called Ponyboy that pet name that he usually reserves for Soda.

Analysis

Chapter 10 begins with the most obvious case of pretending yet: Ponyboy cannot grasp that Johnny has died, so he tells himself, "That still body back in the hospital wasn't Johnny." He pretends that he'll find Johnny at the house, or in the lot. This case of denial has been foreshadowed by Ponyboy's tendency to create alternate realities for himself throughout the story, but the difference is that "this time my dreaming worked. I convinced myself that he wasn't dead."

In Chapter 11, Ponyboy's pretending makes him an unreliable narrator for the first time in the story. When Randy comes to visit, Ponyboy says that he was the one who killed Bob, and that Johnny is not dead. He repeats it aloud to convince himself of it. But, as narrator, he says, "Johnny didn't have anything to do with Bob's getting killed." The reader has depended upon Ponyboy's narration to dictate the events of the story, and now the frame of reference is thrown off, since we know he has moved into an alternate reality.

Dally plans for the police to kill him; Ponyboy knows he's only bluffing when he pulls out his gun, but the goal is for the police to shoot back. His death makes Ponyboy realize that although Johnny appears a hero while Dally appears a hoodlum, Dally was heroic, too. The appearance of the whole situation is much like the Greasers' appearance in general: misleading.

Ponyboy links Johnny and Dally's deaths to *Gone with the Wind*, as he considers how they "died gallant." When Darry tells him that Johnny has left him his copy of the book, Ponyboy can only think of "Southern gentlemen with big black eyes in blue jeans and T-shirts, Southern gentlemen crumpling under street lights."

When Ponyboy wakes up momentarily, he asks Soda if Darry is sorry he's sick. He also worries throughout the chapter that maybe he didn't ask for Darry while he was delirious, but Soda finally confirms that he did. This concern for Darry's feelings represents a huge change from the way Ponyboy regarded his oldest brother in the beginning of the novel. The bond between Ponyboy and Darry is further solidified at the end of Chapter 11, when Darry calls him "little buddy," a nickname he usually reserves for only Soda.

Eyes continue to feature prominently in these chapters. Although Soda is exhausted at the end of Chapter 10, "his dark eyes were still laughing and carefree and reckless;" that part of his personality cannot be conquered. As Ponyboy wonders about Bob Sheldon's personality for the first time, he considers what his eyes might have been like: "maybe brown, like Soda's, maybe dark-blue, like the Shepard boys'. Maybe he'd had black eyes. Like Johnny."

Summary and Analysis of Chapter 12

Summary

Chapter 12 begins with the hearing. Ponyboy listens to Randy, Cherry, and the other Socs testify, all the while feeling frustrated that they keep saying Johnny killed Bob. At this point, he has totally convinced himself that he was the one who committed the murder. Darry and Soda also testify, and tell the judge that Dally was a good friend of theirs, even though that association with a perceived hoodlum will risk their credibility. When it is Ponyboy's chance to be questioned, the judge steers clear of questions about Bob's death. In the end, the judge acquits Ponyboy and the case is closed.

But Ponyboy becomes extremely absent-minded after the hearing. He is disturbed, and his grades begin to drop. His English teacher approaches him and tells him he's failing class, but if he can write a good semester theme, he will get a C, "taking into consideration the circumstances." The English teacher says the theme should be on "anything you think is important enough to write about." Ponyboy reacts sarcastically, although he is polite to the teacher, and leaves.

At lunch, Ponyboy drives to the grocery store with Two-Bit and Steve, and hangs out smoking a cigarette on the fender of Steve's car while the other two are inside. A car full of Socs pulls up, but Ponyboy doesn't feel scared - he doesn't feel anything atll, even when one of them accuses him of killing Bob Sheldon and threatens him. He breaks off the end of his bottle and says, "You get back into your car or you'll get split," scaring the Socs off.

Two-Bit has seen the whole thing, and asks Ponyboy if he really would have used the broken bottle as a weapon; Ponyboy says he would have. Two-Bit says, "Ponyboy, listen, don't get tough. You're not like the rest of us and don't try to be..." but then he grins because he notices that Ponyboy is picking up the pieces of broken bottle from the ground to avoid people getting flat tires.

When Ponyboy gets home, he tries to write the theme for English class, but he is easily distracted and can't concentrate. Soda comes home and has a cigarette, which tips Ponyboy off that something is wrong, since Soda hardly ever smokes. But when Ponyboy asks him if something is wrong, he shakes his head. But after supper, Darry and Ponyboy get into a spat about Ponyboy's grades, which have dropped significantly. But Darry says that "schoolwork's not the point. You're living in a vacuum, Pony, and you're going to have to cut it out." He says that they're all upset about losing Johnny and Dallas, but that Ponyboy has to come back to reality.

When Ponyboy looks at how Soda is reacting to the fight, he sees that his face is white. Then Soda runs out the door, dropping an envelope. It is the letter he wrote to Sandy, returned unopened. Ponyboy realizes that Soda has his own problems, but

Ponyboy has been too wrapped up in himself to notice them, or to listen if Soda has tried to talk about them. Darry and Ponyboy decide to go after Soda, and chase him into the park; Ponyboy tackles him, knocking them both over.

Soda confesses how upset it makes him when Darry and Ponyboy fight. He says that all they have is each other, and that they need to stick together in order not to end up the way Dally was before he died, hardened. Darry and Ponyboy agree not to fight anymore, suddenly realizing how much they accidentally have been hurting Soda. The brothers race back to the house.

Ponyboy finally picks up the copy of *Gone with the Wind* that Johnny left to him, and lets it sink in that Johnny was the one who killed Bob, and that Johnny is now dead. A note from Johnny falls out of the book. Among other things, it says:

> I've been thinking about it, and that poem, that guy that wrote it, he meant you're gold when you're a kid, like green. When you're a kid everything's new, dawn. It's just when you get used to everything that it's day. Like the way you dig sunsets, Pony. That's gold. Keep that way, it's a good way to be.

It also instructs him to tell Dally, but it's too late now. Ponyboy realizes that Dally has died because he let his gold fade, but that it doesn't have to be that way for all the Greasers and disadvantaged people.

So Ponyboy calls Mr. Syme, his English teacher, and asks if his theme can be longer than five pages. When he gets permission, he begins to think about how to start the story, and decides to begin with "When I stepped out into the bright sunlight from the darkness of the movie house, I had only two things on my mind: Paul Newman and a ride home..." which is the opening of *The Outsiders* itself.

Analysis

Although Ponyboy became an unreliable narrator at the end of Chapter 11, when it was clear he was in denial over Johnny's death, he redeems himself as trustworthy to the reader at the very beginning of Chapter 12, by distinguishing Ponyboy the narrator from Ponyboy the character in the story. He explains that the doctor had a talk with the judge before the hearing, and "I didn't know what he had to do with it then, but I do now."

Now that Ponyboy has separated himself as narrator from the character in the story, he uses direct address frequently. He has used it in the past, but now the reader realizes that Ponyboy in the present, the narrator, is in a different emotional state than the Ponyboy in the story. He uses phrases like, "And you know what?" and "I know I don't talk good English (have you ever seen a hood that did?)," directly addressing the reader. The formalism this split induces - of a story-within-the-story and a narrator doubling back on himself - suggests a mise-en-abime that temporarily shifts the emphasis from the narrative to the question of storytelling: we are now aware of that which lies outside the ostensible "story", so that, as those events come to a head, they in turn lose some of their dramatic force.

Johnny's last words, "Stay gold," echo in this chapter when Ponyboy breaks a bottle to defend himself against the Socs. Two-Bit says, "Ponyboy, listen, don't get tough. You're not like the rest of us and don't try to be..." Ponyboy is confused by what Two-Bit means, since he felt nothing when the Socs approached him. But he proves that he is still "gold" by bending down to pick up the pieces of broken glass from the ground without even thinking about it.

Ponyboy and Darry's relationship is once again redefined in this chapter, this time in terms of how it affects Sodapop. He is so upset by the way they always fight that he runs away. They feel selfish for not having realized the effects of their actions on others. Soda argues: "We're all we've got left. We ought to be able to stick together against everything. If we don't have each other, we don't have anything." This idea rings true with Darry and Ponyboy, and finally it is Soda who brings them together.

The various strands - formal and narrative - are tied together in the closing sentences, as the novel ends as it began. The circle is satisfying for its symmetry, but seems to run against Ponyboy's assertion that he has moved on and wants to use his tale to help others. Instead, we are left with the impression of a closed loop, an inexorable tide, a vicious circle that allows no escape. Hinton closes her novel with hope, yes, but also an intimation of its opposite.

Suggested Essay Questions

1. **Compare the characters of Bob and Dally.**

On the surface, Bob and Dally couldn't be more different. However, the two boys are linked together by the phrase, "Next time you want a broad, pick up your own kind." Right before the Socs attack Ponyboy and Johnny, in the fight that results in Johnny killing Bob, Bob states the reasoning for the attack. He wants the Greasers to know their place in society, and to stay away from Soc girls. Later, in Chapter 6, Dally echoes Bob's words when he explains that Cherry is acting as a spy for the Greasers, adding: "Man, next time I want a broad I'll pick up my own kind." Ponyboy remembers Bob saying this not even a week before. Both boys are victims of the violence between the Socs and the Greasers, and die before the story is over. They both have violent tendencies, look for fights, and end up losing their lives because of it; more important, both draw ideological lines in the sand.

2. **Discuss the relationship between Johnny and Dally.**

Johnny feels hero-worship toward Dally, and thinks of him as the most gallant of all the gang. Dally wants to protect Johnny and keep him from turning out the way he himself has. As they drive back to the church in Chapter 5, he explains, "You get hardened in jail. I don't want that to happen to you. Like it happened to me..." After Johnny dies, Dally reacts with uncharacteristic emotion. Ponyboy realizes that "Johnny was the only thing Dally loved. And now Johnny was gone."

3. **Discuss the relationship between Ponyboy and Darry, and how it changes over the course of the novel.**

At the beginning of the novel, Ponyboy resents Darry for being too strict and always bothering him for not using his head. He recognizes the sacrifices that Darry has made to raise his two little brothers, but still thinks Darry just doesn't care for him at all.

But in Chapter 5, when Soda and Darry come to the hospital, Ponyboy has a revelation. He sees his oldest brother cry for the first time in years - he didn't even cry at their parents' funeral - and realizes that "Darry did care about me, maybe as much as he cared about Soda, and because he cared he was trying too hard to make something of me." He understands that Darry is terrified of losing another person he loves, and wonders "how I could ever have thought him hard and unfeeling."

In Chapter 10, when Ponyboy wakes up momentarily, he asks Soda if Darry is sorry he's sick. He also worries throughout the chapter that maybe he didn't ask for Darry while he was delirious, but Soda finally confirms that he did. This concern for Darry's feelings is a huge change from the way Ponyboy regarded his oldest brother in the beginning of the novel. Now he is worried that, because deep down he feels he can relate better to Soda, he might have left Darry out in his unconscious babbling.

4. **How do Ponyboy's feelings toward Randy reflect the conflict between the Socs and the Greasers?**

At first, Ponyboy sees Randy as a violent Soc to be avoided; he is Marcia's boyfriend, and is involved in jumping the Greasers. But in Chapter 7, they have a conversation in Randy's car, and Randy explains why he is leaving town instead of attending the rumble. He says, "You can't win, even if you whip us. You'll still be where you were before - at the bottom. And we'll still be the lucky ones with all the breaks. So it doesn't do any good, the fighting and the killing. It doesn't prove a thing. We'll forget it if you win, or if you don't. Greasers will still be greasers and Socs will still be Socs." Ponyboy begins to see Randy as someone who can appreciate sunsets, and feels a connection to him regardless of their different social statuses.

However, in Chapter 11 when Randy comes to visit Ponyboy at home, Ponyboy's denial about Johnny's death and the events leading up to it cause a rift between the two boys again. Ponyboy decides, "He was just like all the rest of the Socs. Cold-blooded and mean."

5. **What do Johnny's last words mean?**

Johnny's last words echo in Chapter 12 when Ponyboy breaks a bottle to defend himself against the Socs. Two-Bit says, "Ponyboy, listen, don't get tough. You're not like the rest of us and don't try to be..." Ponyboy is confused by what Two-Bit means, since he felt nothing when the Socs approached him. But he proves that he is still "gold" by bending down to pick up the pieces of broken glass from the ground without even thinking about it.

6. **How does *Gone with the Wind* represent an ideal for Johnny?**

Johnny puts his last note to Ponyboy inside his copy of *Gone with the Wind*. The gallantry of the Southern gentlemen in the book, who rode to their certain deaths bravely, inspires Johnny and reminds him of Dally. This allows Ponyboy to see Dally in that light, too, and to consider that his death might have been gallant. Johnny dies as a result of rescuing children from the fire in the church, so in that way he lives up to the ideal in *Gone with the Wind*.

7. **What is the difference between Ponyboy the narrator and Ponyboy the character?**

It is always clear that Ponyboy is narrating *The Outsiders* from a point in the future, after the events of the story have taken place. However, this rift between narrator and character becomes definite in Chapter 11, when

Ponyboy's pretending makes him an unreliable narrator for the first time in the story. When Randy comes to visit, Ponyboy says that he was the one who killed Bob, and that Johnny is not dead. He repeats it aloud to convince himself of it. But as narrator, he says, "Johnny didn't have anything to do with Bob's getting killed." The reader has depended upon Ponyboy's narration to dictate the events of the story, and now the frame of reference is thrown off, since we know he has moved into an alternate reality.

8. **Discuss Ponyboy's "dreaming", particularly in regard to Johnny's death.**

Ponyboy's reaction to Johnny's death has been foreshadowed by Ponyboy's tendency to create alternate realities for himself throughout the story, but the difference is that "this time my dreaming worked. I convinced myself that he wasn't dead." Throughout the story, Ponyboy creates these alternate realities in order to cope with situations he feels are unbearable. For instance, in Chapter 3 he dreams of a life in the country, with his parents still alive and Darry kind and caring again. What is important to note is that he concedes that his dreams are only dreams, and that he admits to use them as a mode of escape.

9. **Describe how eyes are used as a characterization technique.**

Ponyboy's view of other characters is often reflected by his interpretation of their eyes. For example, he says that "Darry's eyes are his own. He's got eyes that are like two pieces of pale blue-green ice. They've got a determined set to them, like the rest of him... he would be real handsome if his eyes weren't so cold." Darry's eyes reflect Ponyboy's view of his oldest brother as "hardly human." In contrast, Sodapop's eyes are "dark brown - lively, dancing, recklessly laughing eyes that can be gentle and sympathetic one moment and blazing with anger the next." Johnny is defined by his emotive eyes; the difference between his mother and him is clear to Ponyboy because of their eyes: "Johnnycake's eyes were fearful and sensitive; hers were cheap and hard."

10. **In what way is *The Outsiders* a call to action?**

The Outsiders ends with its own opening sentence, as Ponyboy begins to write his assignment for English class, and it becomes clear that the story the reader has just finished *is* the assignment itself. It is inspired by Johnny's letter to Ponyboy, in which he explains what he meant by his last words: "Stay gold." There is no reason for lives to be cut short because of senseless violence between the Greasers and the Socs. Ponyboy feels called to action by Johnny's note, and wants to save the lives of other hoods who might end up like Dally. In Chapter 12, this goal is underlined:

> "There should be some help, someone should tell them
> before it was too late. Someone should tell their side of
> the story, and maybe people would understand then and

wouldn't be so quick to judge a boy by the amount of hair oil he wore."

Films based on S.E. Hinton's novels

Francis Ford Coppola was convinced to direct *The Outsiders* film by Jo Ellen Misakian, a librarian at Lone Star Jr. High School in Fresno, California, and her students. The film was shot in 1982 and released in 1983. In 2005, Coppola re-released the film as *The Outsiders: The Complete Novel*, and included scenes that would make the movie more faithful to the novel. For example, the beginning scene in which the Socs jump Ponyboy, the court scene, and a conversation between Ponyboy and Mr. Syme at the end were now included.

After reading *The Outsiders*, Coppola also read Hinton's novel *Rumble Fish*, and was inspired to adapt it to film as well. He wrote the screenplay with Hinton while filming *The Outsiders* - on Sundays when they had time off from shooting - and filmed it right after. Many of the same locations were used in both films, as were many of the same cast and crew members. Both films were shot in Tulsa, Oklahoma.

Tex was Hinton's last young adult novel, but the first to be made into a film in 1982. It starred Matt Dillon and Emilio Estevez, both of whom also starred in *The Outsiders*. The film was directed by Tim Hunter and produced by Walt Disney Pictures.

That Was Then, This Is Now was made into a film by Paramount Pictures in 1985, and also starred Emilio Estevez. Estevez wrote the screenplay.

Films based on S.E. Hinton's novels

Author of ClassicNote and Sources

Meghan Joyce, author of ClassicNote. Completed on May 03, 2009, copyright held by GradeSaver.

Updated and revised Damien Chazelle May 31, 2009. Copyright held by GradeSaver.

Jay Daly. Presenting S.E. Hinton. Boston: Twayne Publishers, 1987.

Rachelle Lasky Bilz. Life Is Tough: Guys, Growing Up, and Young Adult Literature. Lanham, MD: Scarecrow Press, 2004.

Deborah Kovacs, Ed.. Meet the Authors: 25 Writers of Upper Elementary and Middle School Books Talk about Their Work. New York: Scholastic, 1996.

"The Outsiders Official Website." 2009-03-31. <http://www.theoutsidersbookandmovie.com>.

S.E. Hinton. "S.E. Hinton." 2007-03-01. 2009-04-04. <http://www.sehinton.com>.

"A Look Inside a Landmark: *The Outsiders*." John S. Simmons. *Censored Books: Critical Viewpoints." Ed. Nicholas Karolides, Lee Burress, John M. Kean. Lanham, MD: Rowman & Littlefield. 2001.*

Quiz 1

1. **Which Greaser likes to watch movies by himself?**
   A. Two-Bit
   B. Ponyboy
   C. Soda
   D. Darry

2. **How did the Curtis boys' parents die?**
   A. In a fire
   B. In an auto wreck
   C. Of old age
   D. Of the flu

3. **Who is Soda's best friend?**
   A. Dally Winston
   B. Two-Bit Mathews
   C. Sandy
   D. Steve Randle

4. **Who never drinks alcohol?**
   A. Soda
   B. Bob Sheldon
   C. Dally
   D. Darry

5. **Who is Soda's girlfriend?**
   A. Cherry
   B. Sylvia
   C. Evie
   D. Sandy

6. **What does Darry do for a job?**
   A. Plays football
   B. Works at the gas station
   C. He's a student
   D. Roofs houses

7. **How old is Ponyboy?**
    A. Twelve
    B. Twenty
    C. Eighteen
    D. Fourteen

8. **Where did Dally Winston used to live?**
    A. Chicago
    B. New York
    C. Nashville
    D. Australia

9. **Which member of the Greaser gang always steals things for fun?**
    A. Two-Bit
    B. Johnny
    C. Soda
    D. Darry

10. **Who harrasses Cherry and Marcia at the drive-in?**
    A. Ponyboy
    B. Bob Sheldon
    C. Dally
    D. Darry

11. **What does Cherry refuse from Dally?**
    A. Popcorn
    B. His jacket
    C. A date
    D. A coke

12. **Who is Cherry's boyfriend?**
    A. Randy Adderson
    B. Two-Bit Mathews
    C. Bob Sheldon
    D. Johnny Cade

13. **Why did Cherry and Marcia tell their boyfriends to leave?**
   A. Because they were hitting on other girls
   B. Because they were drunk
   C. Because they wanted to break up
   D. Because the Greasers came

14. **Who does Ponyboy confide in about what happened to Johnny?**
   A. Two-Bit
   B. Cherry
   C. Steve Randle
   D. Marcia

15. **Who is Sylvia?**
   A. One of Cherry's cheerleading buddies
   B. Dally's sometimes girlfriend
   C. A Soc
   D. Soda's girlfriend

16. **Who is Mickey Mouse?**
   A. Soda's horse
   B. Johnny's imaginary friend
   C. Ponyboy's dog
   D. Darry's nickname for Two-Bit

17. **What do Cherry and Ponyboy have in common?**
   A. They both have dead parents
   B. They both love Dally Winston
   C. They both like the idea of watching sunsets
   D. They both hate Bob Sheldon

18. **What kind of car do the Socs drive?**
   A. A blue mustang
   B. A Porsche
   C. A red Camero
   D. A black truck

19. **Why does Cherry say she never wants to see Dally again?**
    A. Because she hates him
    B. Because he disgusts her
    C. Because he might hurt Bob
    D. Because she could fall in love with him

20. **What is NOT true about Ponyboy's daydream about the country?**
    A. His parents are alive
    B. His mother talks to Dally
    C. Soda has Mickey Mouse back
    D. Darry is still mean

21. **Where do Johnny and Ponyboy accidentally fall asleep?**
    A. In the fountain
    B. In the vacant lot
    C. On the Curtis boys' couch
    D. At Johnny's parents' house

22. **Why does Ponyboy want to run away from home in Chapter 3?**
    A. Because Soda hits him
    B. Because Darry hits him
    C. Because Soda hits Darry
    D. Because Ponyboy wants to

23. **Which is NOT a reason Ponyboy decides to go back home instead of running away?**
    A. Because he misses Soda
    B. Because he is freezing
    C. Because he forgives Darry
    D. Because he is sleepy

24. **Who approaches Ponyboy and Johnny at the fountain in the park?**
    A. Two-Bit
    B. The Socs
    C. Soda
    D. Darry

25. **Who wears scary rings?**
    A. Two-Bit
    B. Bob
    C. Dally
    D. Randy

Quiz 1 Answer Key

1. **(B)** Ponyboy
2. **(B)** In an auto wreck
3. **(D)** Steve Randle
4. **(A)** Soda
5. **(D)** Sandy
6. **(D)** Roofs houses
7. **(D)** Fourteen
8. **(B)** New York
9. **(A)** Two-Bit
10. **(C)** Dally
11. **(D)** A coke
12. **(C)** Bob Sheldon
13. **(B)** Because they were drunk
14. **(B)** Cherry
15. **(B)** Dally's sometimes girlfriend
16. **(A)** Soda's horse
17. **(C)** They both like the idea of watching sunsets
18. **(A)** A blue mustang
19. **(D)** Because she could fall in love with him
20. **(D)** Darry is still mean
21. **(B)** In the vacant lot
22. **(B)** Because Darry hits him
23. **(C)** Because he forgives Darry
24. **(B)** The Socs
25. **(B)** Bob

Quiz 2

1. **Who stabs Bob Sheldon?**
    A. Johnny
    B. Ponyboy
    C. Dally
    D. Randy

2. **Where do Ponyboy and Johnny find Dally?**
    A. At Buck Merril's house
    B. In the vacant lot
    C. At the Curtis boys' house
    D. In the park

3. **Who does Buck Merril like to listen to?**
    A. Hank Williams
    B. The Beatles
    C. The Rolling Stones
    D. Elvis

4. **When Ponyboy and Johnny find Dally, who has cracked his ribs?**
    A. The Socs
    B. Buck Merril
    C. Tim Shepard
    D. Darry

5. **What is the only thing Dally Winston does honestly?**
    A. Fights
    B. Talks to women
    C. Attends school
    D. Rides ponies

6. **What does Dally NOT give Johnny and Ponyboy?**
    A. A jacket
    B. Some money
    C. Food
    D. A gun

7. How do Johnny and Ponyboy get to Windrixville?

A. They take a cab
B. They walk
C. Dally drives them
D. They jump on a train

8. Which member of the Greaser gang does NOT clown around in church?

A. Two-Bit
B. Ponyboy
C. Soda
D. Steve Randle

9. How do the Greasers identify themselves to each other?

A. By firing their guns
B. With a code word
C. With a long, low whistle
D. With a shout

10. What does Johnny NOT pick up at the store?

A. Matches
B. Baloney
C. I[Gone with the Wind]
D. Hamburgers

11. Who has to bleach his hair?

A. Johnny
B. Ponyboy
C. Soda
D. Dally

12. Who do the Southern gentlemen in I[Gone with the Wind] remind Johnny of?

A. Himself
B. Ponyboy
C. Dally
D. Darry

13. **Who wrote the poem that Ponyboy recites to Johnny?**
   A. Lord Tennyson
   B. Maya Angelou
   C. Ralph Waldo Emerson
   D. Robert Frost

14. **What do Johnny and Ponyboy subsist on while they stay in the church?**
   A. Turkey
   B. Baloney
   C. Sausages
   D. Peanut butter and jelly

15. **Who comes to find Johnny and Ponyboy in the church?**
   A. Cherry
   B. Soda
   C. Dally
   D. Darry

16. **Who gives Dally a letter to give to Ponyboy?**
   A. Two-Bit
   B. Cherry
   C. Soda
   D. Darry

17. **What has Dally told the cops about Johnny and Ponyboy?**
   A. That they are in the abandoned church
   B. That they are hiding in the vacant lot
   C. That they are heading for Texas
   D. That they have left the country

18. **Where does Dally take Johnny and Ponyboy?**
   A. To Dairy Queen
   B. To the hospital
   C. To a grocery store
   D. To an upscale restaurant

19. **Who is spying on the Socs for the Greasers?**
    A. Cherry Valance
    B. Randy Adderson
    C. Sandy
    D. Marcia

20. **Who decides that the boys should turn themselves in for murder?**
    A. Johnny
    B. Ponyboy
    C. Dally
    D. Darry

21. **Who was NOT having a picnic at the church when it caught on fire?**
    A. Schoolchildren
    B. Jerry Wood
    C. Mrs. O'Brient
    D. Ponyboy and Johnny

22. **Why doesn't Jerry Wood follow Ponyboy and Johnny into the church?**
    A. He doesn't want to help the children.
    B. He is too scared.
    C. He is busy fighting with Dally.
    D. He is too fat to fit through the window.

23. **What does Ponyboy think started the fire?**
    A. One of his cigarettes
    B. A forest fire that got out of control
    C. A campfire nearby
    D. The children playing with fire

24. **Who is the last to escape from the church?**
    A. Johnny
    B. Ponyboy
    C. Jerry Wood
    D. Dally

25. **Why did Dally hit Ponyboy across the back when he escapes from the church?**
   A. Because he thought Ponyboy killed Johnny.
   B. Because he is still angry from the carride.
   C. Because Dally was mad that he went in in the first place.
   D. Because his back was on fire.

Quiz 2 Answer Key

1. **(A)** Johnny
2. **(A)** At Buck Merril's house
3. **(A)** Hank Williams
4. **(C)** Tim Shepard
5. **(D)** Rides ponies
6. **(C)** Food
7. **(D)** They jump on a train
8. **(B)** Ponyboy
9. **(C)** With a long, low whistle
10. **(D)** Hamburgers
11. **(B)** Ponyboy
12. **(C)** Dally
13. **(D)** Robert Frost
14. **(B)** Baloney
15. **(C)** Dally
16. **(C)** Soda
17. **(C)** That they are heading for Texas
18. **(A)** To Dairy Queen
19. **(A)** Cherry Valance
20. **(A)** Johnny
21. **(D)** Ponyboy and Johnny
22. **(D)** He is too fat to fit through the window.
23. **(A)** One of his cigarettes
24. **(A)** Johnny
25. **(D)** Because his back was on fire.

Quiz 3

1. **Who rides in the ambulance with Ponyboy?**
   A. Johnny
   B. Jerry Wood
   C. Soda
   D. Dally

2. **Why does Jerry Wood think Ponyboy shouldn't smoke?**
   A. Because there are children around.
   B. Because he's too young.
   C. Because he has just been in an accident.
   D. Because there is a no smoking sign.

3. **Who fools around with the reporters in the hospital waiting room?**
   A. Two-Bit
   B. Ponyboy
   C. Soda
   D. Dally

4. **What is Ponyboy's answer when the reporter asks him "What would you do right now if you could do anything you wanted?"**
   A. "Read I[Gone with the Wind.]"
   B. "Take a bath."
   C. "Go to Disney World."
   D. "Help Johnny."

5. **What is Johnny NOT suffering from?**
   A. Pneumonia
   B. Third-degree burns
   C. A broken back
   D. Severe shock

6. **What happens when Two-Bit spins Ponyboy around in the kitchen?**
   A. The eggs break.
   B. It is very painful, since Ponyboy has third-degree burns.
   C. Ponyboy screams.
   D. He drops him.

7. What is Johnny charged with?
A. Manslaughter
B. Second-degree murder
C. Breaking and entering
D. First-degree murder

8. What sport does Ponyboy play?
A. Soccer
B. Bowling
C. Football
D. Track

9. What is Ponyboy's recurring nightmare about?
A. He can never remember
B. Falling
C. Being brutally beaten by the Socs
D. His mom and dad dying

10. Who sleeps in the same bed with Ponyboy?
A. Two-Bit
B. Johnny
C. Soda
D. Darry

11. Where did Sandy go while Ponyboy and Johnny were gone?
A. To get married to an older man
B. To boarding school
C. To Florida to live with her grandmother
D. To Europe with her parents

12. When Darry has to go to work, who offers to baby-sit Ponyboy?
A. Two-Bit
B. Jerry Wood
C. Soda
D. Steve Randle

13. **What is the Curtis boys' favorite thing to eat for breakfast?**
    A. Eggs benedict
    B. Chocolate cake
    C. Omelettes
    D. Cereal

14. **Who does Ponyboy talk to at the Tasty Freeze on the way to the hospital?**
    A. Dally Winston
    B. Cherry Valance
    C. Randy Adderson
    D. Sandy

15. **What weakness does Randy see in Bob's parents?**
    A. They spoiled Bob
    B. They were never around
    C. They beat him with belts
    D. They abandoned their son

16. **Who decides to leave town instead of going to the rumble?**
    A. Johnny
    B. Bob
    C. Dally
    D. Randy

17. **What does Two-Bit leave the hospital to buy for Johnny?**
    A. A new copy of I[Gone with the Wind.]
    B. Cigarettes
    C. An ice cream sundae
    D. Some baloney

18. **Who comes to see Johnny, but is turned away?**
    A. Two-Bit
    B. Ponyboy
    C. His father
    D. His mother

19. **What is the main characteristic that distinguishes Johnny from his mother?**
    A. The color of his eyes
    B. The emotion in his eyes
    C. His straight black hair
    D. He is much littler

20. **What does Johnny's mother do when she sees Ponyboy and Two-Bit in the hospital?**
    A. Tells them it's their fault Johnny is dying
    B. Hugs them
    C. Screams nonsense words
    D. Starts crying uncontrollably

21. **What does Two-Bit give to Dally?**
    A. His switchblade
    B. A gun
    C. Cigarettes
    D. A copy of I[Gone with the Wind.]

22. **How do Ponyboy and Two-Bit get home from the hospital?**
    A. They walk
    B. A bus
    C. Two-Bit's car
    D. Hitch-hiking

23. **Why doesn't Cherry want to go see Johnny?**
    A. Because he killed Bob
    B. Because she's afraid she will fall in love with him
    C. Because she hates the hospital
    D. Because she feels guilty

24. **What color are Cherry Valance's eyes?**
    A. Blue
    B. Green
    C. Hazel
    D. Brown

25. Who likes to fight because it's full of action?

    A. Ponyboy

    B. Soda

    C. Dally

    D. Darry

Quiz 3 Answer Key

1. **(B)** Jerry Wood
2. **(B)** Because he's too young.
3. **(C)** Soda
4. **(B)** "Take a bath."
5. **(A)** Pneumonia
6. **(A)** The eggs break.
7. **(A)** Manslaughter
8. **(D)** Track
9. **(A)** He can never remember
10. **(C)** Soda
11. **(C)** To Florida to live with her grandmother
12. **(A)** Two-Bit
13. **(B)** Chocolate cake
14. **(C)** Randy Adderson
15. **(A)** They spoiled Bob
16. **(D)** Randy
17. **(A)** A new copy of I[Gone with the Wind.]
18. **(D)** His mother
19. **(B)** The emotion in his eyes
20. **(A)** Tells them it's their fault Johnny is dying
21. **(A)** His switchblade
22. **(B)** A bus
23. **(A)** Because he killed Bob
24. **(B)** Green
25. **(B)** Soda

Quiz 4

1. **What game did Curly Shepard and Ponyboy once hurt each other playing?**
   A. Chicken
   B. Checkers
   C. Football
   D. Chess

2. **Why isn't Curly Shepard at the rumble?**
   A. Because he is in the hospital
   B. Because he stayed home scared
   C. Because he's in the reformatory
   D. Because he ran away from town, tired of all the fighting

3. **Who likes to fight because everyone else is doing it?**
   A. Two-Bit
   B. Ponyboy
   C. Dally
   D. Darry

4. **Who does one of the Brumly guys identify to Ponyboy as the probable leader of their gang?**
   A. Ponyboy himself
   B. Soda
   C. Dally
   D. Darry

5. **Who used to play football with Darry?**
   A. Curly Shepard
   B. Dally Winston
   C. Paul Holden
   D. Tim Shepard

6. **Who throws the first punch of the rumble?**
   A. Randy Adderson
   B. Paul Holden
   C. Dally
   D. Darry

7. **How did Dally get out of the hospital?**
   A. He threatened a nurse with Two-Bit's switchblade
   B. He pretended to have a nervous breakdown
   C. The doctor said he was recovered and could leave
   D. He climbed out a window

8. **After the rumble, who drives Ponyboy to the hospital to see Johnny?**
   A. Two-Bit
   B. Randy Adderson
   C. Dally
   D. Darry

9. **What does Dally tell the police officer who pulls them over?**
   A. That Ponyboy is sick and they are going to the hospital
   B. Nothing; he doesn't stop driving
   C. That they need to get to the hospital to visit Johnny
   D. To leave them alone

10. **How does Ponyboy get home from the hospital after Johnny dies?**
    A. The bus
    B. He walks
    C. Dally drives him
    D. A stranger gives him a ride

11. **What does Dally tell Darry on the phone?**
    A. That he is running away and never coming back
    B. That he has robbed a grocery store and the cops are after him
    C. That he is broken up over Johnny's death
    D. That Ponyboy is sick

12. **How does Dally die?**
    A. He shoots himself in the head.
    B. The cops shoot him because he pulls out a gun.
    C. The Socs beat him up in the rumble.
    D. He dies of his injuries in the fire.

13. What does Johnny leave Ponyboy?

    A. His hair grease

    B. His copy of I[Gone with the Wind.]

    C. His favorite switchblade

    D. A pack of cigarettes

14. What does Darry make for Ponyboy when he wakes up?

    A. Mushroom soup

    B. Chocolate cake

    C. Eggs

    D. An ice cream sundae

15. Whose picture does Ponyboy study in the yearbook?

    A. Dally Winston

    B. Randy Adderson

    C. Bob Sheldon

    D. Darry

16. Who comes to visit Ponyboy when he is bedridden?

    A. Mr. Syme

    B. Cherry Valance

    C. Randy Adderson

    D. Marcia

17. What does Ponyboy convince himself of regarding Bob's death?

    A. That he killed Bob, not Johnny

    B. That it was purely an accident

    C. That it was another Soc who stabbed him

    D. That it was the cops' fault

18. Why does Darry scold Ponyboy after Randy leaves their house?

    A. Because he is in denial about Johnny's death

    B. Because he stayed out late the night before

    C. Because he hasn't eaten anything

    D. Because he is smoking in bed

19. **Who is NOT questioned at the court hearing?**
   A. Cherry
   B. Ponyboy
   C. Randy
   D. Steve Randle

20. **What does NOT happen to Ponyboy after the hearing?**
   A. He loses his appetite
   B. He starts failing his classes
   C. He starts excelling on the track team
   D. He becomes absent-minded

21. **How does Ponyboy react when the Socs accost him (over killing their friend in the grocery store parking lot)?**
   A. He feels terrified, like Johnny would have
   B. He screams for Two-Bit and Steve
   C. He feels nothing, and breaks a bottle to scare them off
   D. He feels incredibly angry

22. **How does Ponyboy know something is bothering Soda?**
   A. He smokes a cigarette
   B. He drinks a beer
   C. He tries to pick a fight
   D. He doesn't come home after work

23. **Why is Soda so upset?**
   A. Because they lost the rumble
   B. Because he hates when Ponyboy smokes in bed
   C. Because Ponyboy's grades are failing
   D. Because the letter he wrote to Sandy was sent back unopened

24. **What is inside the copy of I[Gone with the Wind]?**
   A. A note from the doctor
   B. Some money
   C. A note from Johnny
   D. A baloney sandwich

25. **What does Ponyboy call Mr. Syme to ask?**
    A. If he can write the theme about his own life
    B. If he can get out of writing the theme
    C. If the theme can be longer than required
    D. Why his grades are failing

Quiz 4 Answer Key

1. **(A)** Chicken
2. **(C)** Because he's in the reformatory
3. **(A)** Two-Bit
4. **(D)** Darry
5. **(C)** Paul Holden
6. **(B)** Paul Holden
7. **(A)** He threatened a nurse with Two-Bit's switchblade
8. **(C)** Dally
9. **(A)** That Ponyboy is sick and they are going to the hospital
10. **(D)** A stranger gives him a ride
11. **(B)** That he has robbed a grocery store and the cops are after him
12. **(B)** The cops shoot him because he pulls out a gun.
13. **(B)** His copy of I[Gone with the Wind.]
14. **(A)** Mushroom soup
15. **(C)** Bob Sheldon
16. **(C)** Randy Adderson
17. **(A)** That he killed Bob, not Johnny
18. **(D)** Because he is smoking in bed
19. **(D)** Steve Randle
20. **(C)** He starts excelling on the track team
21. **(C)** He feels nothing, and breaks a bottle to scare them off
22. **(A)** He smokes a cigarette
23. **(D)** Because the letter he wrote to Sandy was sent back unopened
24. **(C)** A note from Johnny
25. **(C)** If the theme can be longer than required

ClassicNotes

GradeSaver™

Getting you the grade since 1999™

Other ClassicNotes from GradeSaver™

1984
Absalom, Absalom
Adam Bede
The Adventures of Augie March
The Adventures of Huckleberry Finn
The Adventures of Tom Sawyer
The Aeneid
Agamemnon
The Age of Innocence
The Alchemist (Coelho)
The Alchemist (Jonson)
Alice in Wonderland
All My Sons
All Quiet on the Western Front
All the King's Men
All the Pretty Horses
Allen Ginsberg's Poetry
The Ambassadors
American Beauty
And Then There Were None
Angela's Ashes
Animal Farm
Anna Karenina
Anthem
Antigone
Antony and Cleopatra
Aristotle's Ethics
Aristotle's Poetics
Aristotle's Politics
As I Lay Dying
As You Like It

Astrophil and Stella
Atlas Shrugged
Atonement
The Awakening
Babbitt
The Bacchae
Bartleby the Scrivener
The Bean Trees
The Bell Jar
Beloved
Benito Cereno
Beowulf
Bhagavad-Gita
Billy Budd
Black Boy
Bleak House
Bless Me, Ultima
Blindness
Blood Wedding
The Bloody Chamber
Bluest Eye
The Bonfire of the Vanities
The Book of the Duchess and Other Poems
The Book Thief
Brave New World
Breakfast at Tiffany's
Breakfast of Champions
The Brief Wondrous Life of Oscar Wao
The Brothers Karamazov
The Burning Plain and Other Stories
A Burnt-Out Case
By Night in Chile

Call of the Wild
Candide
The Canterbury Tales
Cat on a Hot Tin Roof
Cat's Cradle
Catch-22
The Catcher in the Rye
The Caucasian Chalk Circle
Charlotte Temple
Charlotte's Web
The Cherry Orchard
The Chocolate War
The Chosen
A Christmas Carol
Christopher Marlowe's Poems
Chronicle of a Death Foretold
Civil Disobedience
Civilization and Its Discontents
A Clockwork Orange
Coleridge's Poems
The Color of Water
The Color Purple
Comedy of Errors
Communist Manifesto
A Confederacy of Dunces
Confessions
Connecticut Yankee in King Arthur's Court
The Consolation of Philosophy
Coriolanus

For our full list of over 250 Study Guides, Quizzes,
Sample College Application Essays, Literature Essays and E-texts, visit:

www.gradesaver.com

ClassicNotes

GradeSaver™

Getting you the grade since 1999™

Other ClassicNotes from GradeSaver™

The Count of Monte
  Cristo
The Country Wife
Crime and Punishment
The Crucible
Cry, the Beloved
  Country
The Crying of Lot 49
The Curious Incident of
  the Dog in the
  Night-time
Cymbeline
Daisy Miller
David Copperfield
Death in Venice
Death of a Salesman
The Death of Ivan Ilych
Democracy in America
Devil in a Blue Dress
Dharma Bums
The Diary of a Young
  Girl by Anne Frank
Disgrace
Divine Comedy-I:
  Inferno
Do Androids Dream of
  Electric Sheep?
Doctor Faustus
  (Marlowe)
A Doll's House
Don Quixote Book I
Don Quixote Book II
Dora: An Analysis of a
  Case of Hysteria
Dr. Jekyll and Mr. Hyde
Dracula

Dubliners
East of Eden
Electra by Sophocles
The Electric Kool-Aid
  Acid Test
Emily Dickinson's
  Collected Poems
Emma
Ender's Game
Endgame
The English Patient
The Epic of Gilgamesh
Ethan Frome
The Eumenides
Everyman: Morality Play
Everything is Illuminated
The Faerie Queene
Fahrenheit 451
The Fall of the House of
  Usher
A Farewell to Arms
The Federalist Papers
Fences
Flags of Our Fathers
Flannery O'Connor's
  Stories
For Whom the Bell Tolls
The Fountainhead
Frankenstein
Franny and Zooey
The Giver
The Glass Castle
The Glass Menagerie
The God of Small Things
Goethe's Faust
The Good Earth

The Good Woman of
  Setzuan
The Grapes of Wrath
Great Expectations
The Great Gatsby
Grendel
The Guest
Gulliver's Travels
Hamlet
The Handmaid's Tale
Hard Times
Haroun and the Sea of
  Stories
Harry Potter and the
  Philosopher's Stone
Heart of Darkness
Hedda Gabler
Henry IV (Pirandello)
Henry IV Part 1
Henry IV Part 2
Henry V
Herzog
Hippolytus
The Hobbit
Homo Faber
House of Mirth
The House of the Seven
  Gables
The House of the Spirits
House on Mango Street
How the Garcia Girls
  Lost Their Accents
Howards End
A Hunger Artist
I Know Why the Caged
  Bird Sings

For our full list of over 250 Study Guides, Quizzes,
Sample College Application Essays, Literature Essays and E-texts, visit:

www.gradesaver.com

ClassicNotes

GrAdeSaver™

Getting you the grade since 1999™

Other ClassicNotes from GradeSaver™

I, Claudius
An Ideal Husband
Iliad
The Importance of Being
   Earnest
In Cold Blood
In Our Time
In the Time of the
   Butterflies
Inherit the Wind
An Inspector Calls
Interpreter of Maladies
Into the Wild
Invisible Man
The Island of Dr. Moreau
Jane Eyre
Jazz
The Jew of Malta
Joseph Andrews
The Joy Luck Club
Julius Caesar
The Jungle
Jungle of Cities
Kama Sutra
Kate Chopin's Short
   Stories
Kidnapped
King Lear
King Solomon's Mines
The Kite Runner
Last of the Mohicans
Leaves of Grass
The Legend of Sleepy
   Hollow
A Lesson Before Dying
Leviathan

Libation Bearers
Life is Beautiful
Life of Pi
Light In August
Like Water for Chocolate
The Lion, the Witch and
   the Wardrobe
Little Women
Lolita
Long Day's Journey Into
   Night
Look Back in Anger
Lord Jim
Lord of the Flies
The Lord of the Rings:
   The Fellowship of the
   Ring
The Lord of the Rings:
   The Return of the
   King
The Lord of the Rings:
   The Two Towers
A Lost Lady
The Lottery and Other
   Stories
Love in the Time of
   Cholera
The Love Song of J.
   Alfred Prufrock
The Lovely Bones
Lucy
Macbeth
Madame Bovary
Maggie: A Girl of the
   Streets and Other
   Stories

Manhattan Transfer
Mankind: Medieval
   Morality Plays
Mansfield Park
The Marrow of Tradition
The Master and
   Margarita
MAUS
The Mayor of
   Casterbridge
Measure for Measure
Medea
Merchant of Venice
Metamorphoses
The Metamorphosis
Middlemarch
A Midsummer Night's
   Dream
Moby Dick
A Modest Proposal and
   Other Satires
Moll Flanders
Mother Courage and Her
   Children
Mrs. Dalloway
Much Ado About
   Nothing
My Antonia
Mythology
The Namesake
Native Son
Nickel and Dimed: On
   (Not) Getting By in
   America
Night
Nine Stories

For our full list of over 250 Study Guides, Quizzes,
Sample College Application Essays, Literature Essays and E-texts, visit:

www.gradesaver.com

ClassicNotes

GradeSaver™

Getting you the grade since 1999™

Other ClassicNotes from GradeSaver™

No Exit
Northanger Abbey
Notes from Underground
O Pioneers
The Odyssey
Oedipus Rex or Oedipus
   the King
Of Mice and Men
The Old Man and the Sea
Oliver Twist
On Liberty
On the Road
One Day in the Life of
   Ivan Denisovich
One Flew Over the
   Cuckoo's Nest
One Hundred Years of
   Solitude
Oroonoko
Oryx and Crake
Othello
Our Town
The Outsiders
Pale Fire
Pamela: Or Virtue
   Rewarded
Paradise Lost
A Passage to India
The Pearl
Percy Shelley: Poems
Perfume: The Story of a
   Murderer
Persepolis: The Story of
   a Childhood
Persuasion
Phaedra

Phaedrus
The Piano Lesson
The Picture of Dorian
   Gray
Poe's Poetry
Poe's Short Stories
Poems of W.B. Yeats:
   The Rose
Poems of W.B. Yeats:
   The Tower
The Poems of William
   Blake
The Poetry of Robert
   Frost
The Poisonwood Bible
Pope's Poems and Prose
Portrait of the Artist as a
   Young Man
Pride and Prejudice
The Prince
The Professor's House
Prometheus Bound
Pudd'nhead Wilson
Pygmalion
Rabbit, Run
A Raisin in the Sun
The Real Life of
   Sebastian Knight
Rebecca
The Red Badge of
   Courage
The Remains of the Day
The Republic
Rhinoceros
Richard II
Richard III

The Rime of the Ancient
   Mariner
Rip Van Winkle and
   Other Stories
The Road
Robinson Crusoe
Roll of Thunder, Hear
   My Cry
Romeo and Juliet
A Room of One's Own
A Room With a View
A Rose For Emily and
   Other Short Stories
Rosencrantz and
   Guildenstern Are
   Dead
Salome
The Scarlet Letter
The Scarlet Pimpernel
The Seagull
Season of Migration to
   the North
Second Treatise of
   Government
The Secret Life of Bees
The Secret River
Secret Sharer
Sense and Sensibility
A Separate Peace
Shakespeare's Sonnets
Shantaram
Short Stories of Ernest
   Hemingway
Short Stories of F. Scott
   Fitzgerald
Siddhartha

For our full list of over 250 Study Guides, Quizzes,
Sample College Application Essays, Literature Essays and E-texts, visit:

www.gradesaver.com

ClassicNotes

Gr_d_eSaver™

Getting you the grade since 1999™

Other ClassicNotes from GradeSaver™

Silas Marner
Sir Gawain and the
  Green Knight
Sister Carrie
Six Characters in Search
  of an Author
Slaughterhouse Five
Snow Falling on Cedars
The Social Contract
Something Wicked This
  Way Comes
Song of Roland
Song of Solomon
Songs of Innocence and
  of Experience
Sons and Lovers
The Sorrows of Young
  Werther
The Sound and the Fury
The Spanish Tragedy
Spenser's Amoretti and
  Epithalamion
Spring Awakening
The Stranger
A Streetcar Named
  Desire
Sula
The Sun Also Rises
Tale of Two Cities
The Taming of the Shrew
The Tempest
Tender is the Night
Tess of the D'Urbervilles
Their Eyes Were
  Watching God
Things Fall Apart

The Things They Carried
A Thousand Splendid
  Suns
The Threepenny Opera
Through the Looking
  Glass
Thus Spoke Zarathustra
The Time Machine
Titus Andronicus
To Build a Fire
To Kill a Mockingbird
To the Lighthouse
The Tortilla Curtain
Touching Spirit Bear
Treasure Island
Trifles
Troilus and Cressida
Tropic of Cancer
Tropic of Capricorn
Tuesdays With Morrie
The Turn of the Screw
Twelfth Night
Twilight
Ulysses
Uncle Tom's Cabin
Utopia
Vanity Fair
A Very Old Man With
  Enormous Wings
Villette
The Visit
Volpone
Waiting for Godot
Waiting for Lefty
Walden
Washington Square

The Waste Land
The Wealth of Nations
Where the Red Fern
  Grows
White Fang
A White Heron and
  Other Stories
White Noise
White Teeth
Who's Afraid of Virginia
  Woolf
Wide Sargasso Sea
Wieland
Winesburg, Ohio
The Winter's Tale
The Woman Warrior
Wordsworth's Poetical
  Works
Woyzeck
A Wrinkle in Time
Wuthering Heights
The Yellow Wallpaper
Yonnondio: From the
  Thirties
Zeitoun

For our full list of over 250 Study Guides, Quizzes,
Sample College Application Essays, Literature Essays and E-texts, visit:

www.gradesaver.com

Made in the USA
Las Vegas, NV
01 April 2021

20602668R00066